CHASING THE SUN

JUANES

CHASING THE SUN

A CELEBRA BOOK

Celebra
Published by the Penguin Group
Penguin Group (USA) Inc., 375 Hudson Street,
New York, New York 10014, USA
Penguin Group (Canada), 90 Eglinton Avenue East, Suite 700, Toronto,
Ontario M4P 2Y3, Canada (a division of Pearson Penguin Canada Inc.)
Penguin Books Ltd., 80 Strand, London WC2R 0RL, England
Penguin Ireland, 25 St. Stephen's Green, Dublin 2,
Ireland (a division of Penguin Books Ltd.)
Penguin Group (Australia), 707 Collins Street, Melbourne, Victoria 3008,
Australia (a division of Pearson Australia Group Pty. Ltd.)
Penguin Books India Pvt. Ltd., 11 Community Centre, Panchsheel Park,
New Delhi–110 017, India
Penguin Group (NZ), 67 Apollo Drive, Rosedale, Auckland 0632,
New Zealand (a division of Pearson New Zealand Ltd.)
Penguin Books (South Africa), Rosebank Office Park, 181 Jan Smuts
Avenue, Parktown North 2193, South Africa
Penguin China, B7 Jiaming Center, 27 East Third Ring Road North,
Chaoyang District, Beijing 100020, China

Penguin Books Ltd., Registered Offices:
80 Strand, London WC2R 0RL, England

First published by Celebra,
a division of Penguin Group (USA) Inc.

First Printing, April 2013
10 9 8 7 6 5 4 3 2 1

LIBRARY OF CONGRESS CATALOGING-IN-PUBLICATION DATA:

Juanes.
Chasing the sun/Juanes.
pages cm
ISBN 978-0-451-41553-0
1. Juanes. 2. Rock musicians—Colombia—Biography.
I. Title.
ML420.J84A3 2013
782.42164092—dc23   2012041976
[B]

Set in Helvetica Neue LT Std
Designed by Pauline Neuwirth

ALWAYS LEARNING   PEARSON

TO LUNA, PALOMA, DANTE, AND KAREN

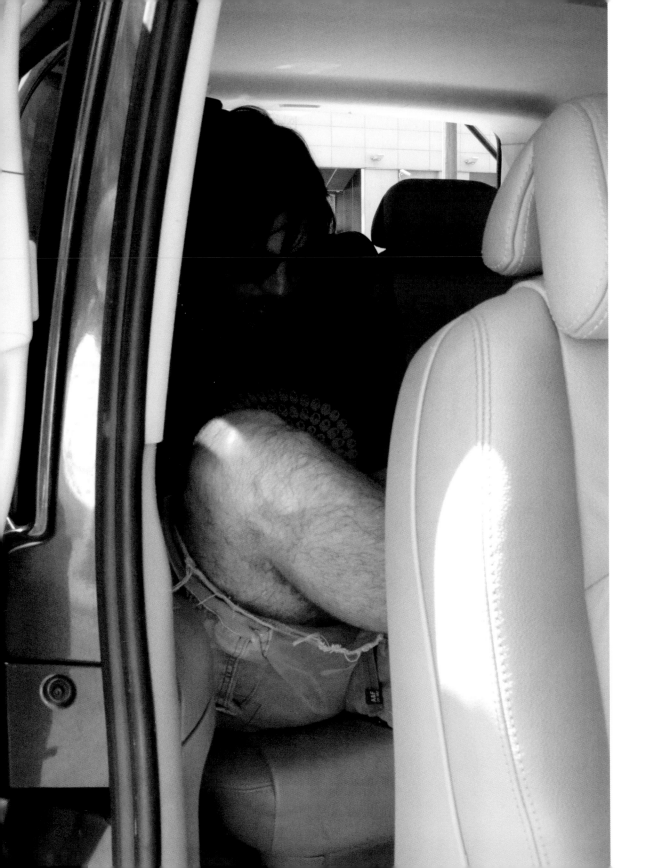

CONTENTS

CHASING THE SUN

INTRODUCTION

Today, as I write these words, we are just starting rehearsals for our next tour, and the best is yet to come. Rehearsals, as always, involve the beautiful adventure of going back to the beginning. The newest chapters in this book have yet to be written; the various untraveled labyrinths of the mind have yet to be discovered. Meanwhile, as the world continues on and as new experiences arise, there will be more material for this book.

But for now, I just want to outline a few memories from my life, and share them as if I were sitting in my living room among friends.

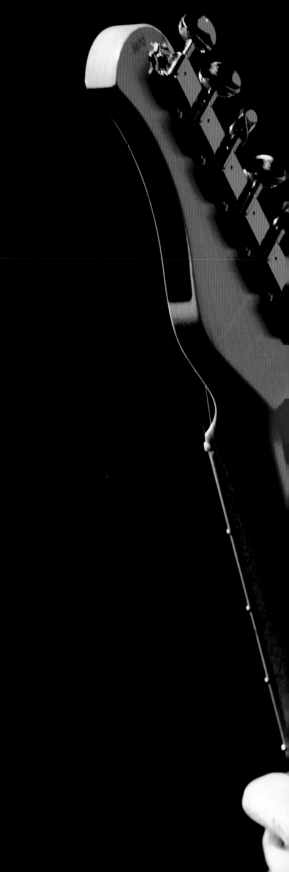

This is an expression of pure friendship and a sincere way of saying thanks to everyone who has supported my music over the years. I'm sure those are the people who have read up to this point. Others might only read certain sections in order to comment or criticize.

It's honestly nothing personal—it's just a fact of life. It's not my job to write books. Not in the least. Since this idea was first proposed to me, I went through a number of stages. I felt that if I really did this, it would be for you to learn who I truly am, who it is behind the songs you hear at the concerts. Why I make the music I make, and why I think the way I think.

I feel it's a risk for someone to expose his soul. In other words, after reading this—or at least after seeing it published—some people might not understand what I'm trying to say. Others will read it and connect even more deeply. Let's just say it's a risk I'm willing to take, and I'll do it with love.

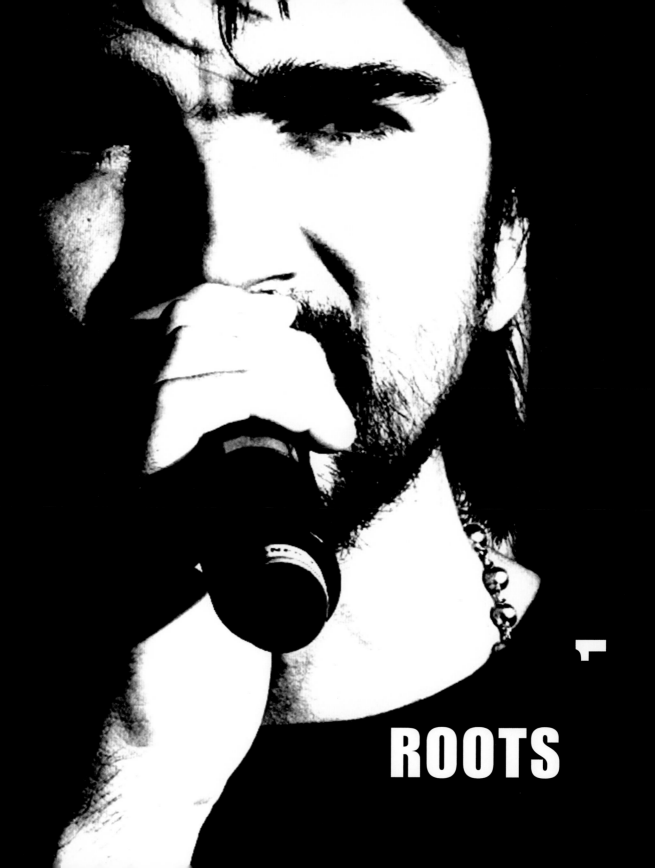

hen I was a child, my mother taught me the value of spirituality, and it has marked my life ever since. I even have a few images stowed away in my mind: kneeling down to pray before going to bed while my brother Jaime slept or watched television.

I was only five years old and would constantly repeat to myself: "As long as God is with me, I will never want for anything, nothing bad will happen to me, and I will always have faith. No matter what happens, no matter the situation . . . I will always have faith." I continue to say that today. Whether in various forms or under different names, I've done this all my life.

As I continued to grow and dream, God was my constant, vital reference point, even in the day-to-day happenings of life. He helped me succeed in school, to feel the strength necessary to go out onstage and sing at school assemblies, and to pass those math tests that always terrified me.

Every week, during religion classes at the Catholic school I attended, we discussed biblical passages with the teacher. My faith was blind and I saw the world only from that point of view. Obviously, that was the only perspective I saw and accepted from my environment, family, and school. Now I'm more aware than ever of the power of the mind, of our capacity to construct and destroy with our thoughts. My entire journey through music and life has been based on yearning, on dreaming, on that blind faith in the universe that makes things happen when you wish for them. From the biggest success to the deepest failure, I've visualized it all in my mind before it comes to pass. Of course there are variations, but in essence I've seen it first, I've imagined it . . .

At night, after dinner, my parents prayed the rosary. I fondly remember those warm, simple nights with the whole family, parents and children sitting at the table. Javier Emilio is the oldest of six siblings and the main reason I'm singing and playing the guitar today. Next came Luz Cecilia, who was always the most diligent and studious, the perfect daughter, until destiny made its cruel-

est judgment and brought it down upon the entire family. Immediately after she gave birth to her daughter, Luz Cecilia suffered internal hemorrhaging that left her in a coma that persists to this day—she's spent twenty years in bed without knowing a thing, if she can feel or hear or see. Looking back, we still can't understand why this happened to her or our family.

Then there's José Luis, perhaps as studious as Luz Cecilia, dedicated to household finances, very reserved and prepared. After him is Mara, or María Victoria, who's been a joyful soul, a horse lover to the end, and one of my closest confidantes—she knows everything (or almost everything) about my life. And Jaime, the finest of all the Aristizabals, an organized and devoted sports fan. Finally, Aunt Adíela rounds out the family that surrounded me in my youth.

All of these people were part of the loveliest moments of my childhood. Now that I'm a father myself, I try to re-create the same sense of closeness with my children, and with my friends and acquaintances as well. "Family is made around the table," I once heard someone say. It's absolutely true! What better place but at home to share the day with the people you love?

When I think back to that time, I always see my dad, Javier Aristizabal, sitting in his chair after having his usual cup of tea—a ritual as sacred as the rosary itself—repeating the Our Father, the Hail Mary, the Glory Be to the Father, the First Mystery, then beginning the exact chorus again in unison with my aunt and mom, who was responsible for keeping the cadence and giving rhythm to the oration. My dear mother, Alicia Vásquez, has always been and continues to be a balm in my life. She is one of those quiet, taciturn women who say little and yet, when they do, speak with such wisdom and honesty. A woman of few words and great truth. Pure goodness. That's my mother.

At first, my siblings and I had to stay at the table until we finished the entire rosary—every night of the week, Monday to Friday, and then on the weekends as well. As we grew up, my siblings— from oldest to youngest—were allowed to leave the table at the start of the oration.

The youngest of the six, I spent the most time at the table—ten years more than Javier, the oldest—and ended up sitting with my parents and aunt Adíela, following the exact same chorus each and every night, with my mom's unmistakable cadence and rhythm. Somehow, I came to understand it as a meditation or a form of disconnecting from reality and entering a sort of trance that empowers everyone present. Today, I see it as one of those magical moments that define our life and which we can only fully appreciate many years later. I feel it's a moment of introspection that goes beyond simply repeating words from memory; to me it's like a moment of silence in which you truly listen to that internal voice that's always speaking to you—the voice that speaks to all of us. I sum up the day or night, I reach a balance, and I put my mind and my faith to work constructing new dreams, new days. What has become a daily exercise has accompanied me, in one form or another, since the tender days of my youth.

Sometimes as I'm stretched out on the floor next to the bed, my wife will call out, "Juan, are you okay?" She asks because it looks like I've passed out on my back, but in fact I do it to meditate. From time to time, an hour or more can pass in which my mind goes a bit crazy, swaying this way and that until it finds the particular shade of white that it seeks.

Like many houses in Latin America, ours was filled with religious images. In fact, when it came to the crucifix hanging in my mother's room, the only thing she didn't do was talk to it. Every time she passed by she would touch it as a means of asking for something or offering her thanks for a blessing received. So I learned to do the very same thing, and every time I was near it, I touched it to ask for a favor or to show my gratitude for a favor received.

Hanging over my bed was a watercolor painting of Jesus that my mom bought for a few dollars from a woman in Carolina del Príncipe, the town where my parents had a country home we'd go to for vacation or on the weekends. That image of Jesus emitted a special sort of energy; there was a great sense of mystery in his gaze, a strange mysticism amid a very dark background. The peculiarity of the image—common in religious paintings—was that I could see Jesus following me with his eyes from whatever angle I stood. I knelt down in front of that painting every night to pray, and there my sense of spirituality and connection with God grew. The painting still exists to this day, and now hangs in my mom's house in Medellín.

■

From a very young age, my imagination was brimming with fantasies, histories, theories, legends, poetry, and reality. Back then, we lived in a house in the center of Medellín not far from Calle Argentina and El Palo. It was a

big house with many rooms and a patio out back. We even had a turtle. I spent my time walking from one end of the house to the other, playing and discovering the world through music, television, and schoolbooks.

My childhood was a happy one, and I grew up surrounded by many family members. I remember my dad and my brothers and sisters singing popular Latin American songs, by Los Hermanos Visconti, Los Chalchaleros, Carlos Gardel, Lucho Gatica, and Julio Jaramillo. Javier, the oldest, was the first to catch the guitar-and-song fever, and we all followed, each in our own unique style.

Javier always sang tangos and music by Los Hermanos Visconti; José preferred songs about broken hearts, Las Hermanitas Calle, an occasional *vallenato*, and *carrilera* music. Jaime sang Francis Cabrel and *la boquitrompona (guasca)*. And finally there was me, crazy about every genre, especially Cuban ballads and music from the south, like *zambas*, *chacareras*, tangos, and the like.

There were always a few guitars lying around the living room, and they caught my attention at a very young age. Three or four on the sofa, the armchair, the table. This always bothered my mom, who would hide them in a corner or behind a curtain so the house wouldn't seem messy, but it was hopeless: the guitars always found their way back out into the open.

It was usually Javier and I who sat down to play songs by ear—by Los Hermanos Visconti, Los Chalchaleros, Julio Jaramillo, and so on—or compose what we could. Javier even paired up with an old friend named Pol, and they called themselves Los Conti, in honor of Los Hermanos Visconti. You can imagine the fanaticism we had in our house for that Argentine folk duo. On some occasions we were all able to get together to sing—Jaime, José, Javier, and myself. I admit there were moments when I got pretty excited, since music united us in a truly incredible way; it was like one of those climactic moments in movies where everything and everyone is at the peak of happiness. There are a few pictures of me playing music with my brothers when I was eight years old and could barely wrap my arms around the guitar because it was bigger than me.

One day when I was home from school with the chicken pox, I went into José's room and found a beautiful harp buried under some clothes and shoes in his closet. It was a woody color and was missing a few strings, and it had some thick wool yarn wrapped around the head and soundboard, which was often how it was used by student bands. I took it out, laid it on the bed, and dusted it off. It looked like it hadn't been used in several years. I think it belonged to my aunt Pastora (who wasn't a shepherdess, even though that's how her name translates) from her days playing in a neighborhood group. I traced my fingers across the strings and that alone was enough to create a sound that drove me absolutely wild.

It was love at first sight. For years, I'd felt a special attraction to music through my father and

brothers, who never passed up a chance to sing. The feeling I had when I touched the harp for the first time represented a direct connection between music and myself. I didn't know a single chord, but the pure sound of those strings drew me in and left my head spinning. Needless to say, it didn't go back into the closet!

After that, my brothers and I started taking guitar lessons from Gabriel Cañas, our official instructor. He was a wonderful guy with a thick beard and he always greeted us with an abundance of joy. He was left-handed, so his guitar was strung backward—that is, it was backward for me, just as he surely thought my guitar was backward for him . . . His place was located in the heart of the city, just a few blocks from my house. There was just enough space for him, one of my brothers, myself, our guitars, and that was it. I'd sit down in front and we'd get started.

After school, I was taken to my guitar lessons by Ana Pérez, one of the most beloved people in my life and who—even after her departure over twenty years ago—I still think of with the same great sense of affection, for she was always at my mother's side helping to raise the entire Aristizabal clan. When I would arrive at my lessons, I remember Gabriel asking, "Juanes, what have you brought to learn today?" I always had a tape of one song or another that I wanted to learn, usually by Los Hermanos Visconti. I sang the first one I learned, "Zamba de Mi Esperanza," at an endless number of school assemblies. Other songs from those days included "Mis Harapos," "India," "Zapo Cancionero," "Ódiame," and countless others of that sort.

I was around eight years old when I went to my first concert. It was at the Pablo Tobón Uribe theater and Los Hermanos Visconti were appearing with special guests Dueto de Antaño. I still remember where my seats were, and the feeling of shock in my stomach at seeing live music for the first time. Dueto de Antaño came onstage first, playing "Pañuelito Blanco," one of those lovely little songs that my dad sang incessantly. And then came the main attraction: Los Hermanos Visconti.

I remember the lyrics, the stage lights, the happy crowd . . . it was pure emotion, pure feeling. I couldn't believe I was seeing the songs I sang at home with my brothers being performed live. The sound of Abel's guitar and Victor's powerful voice had me completely entranced. When they were done playing, we were allowed backstage to meet the band. It was an unbelievable experience for me, just as it would be for my daughters to meet Justin Bieber or Demi Lovato. Back then I was a fan of pop music, which meant Los Hermanos Visconti were idols to me. To this day, I still have the autographed photo we took together.

I was so impressed with the performance that I asked my aunt Pastora to please make me a gaucho costume like the ones worn by Los Hermanos Visconti and Los Chalchaleros. All I wanted was to be more like them.

From that moment on, I stepped up my guitar lessons and focused on developing my musical ear. When everyone else in the house was asleep, I'd sit in the living room all alone to practice and listen to songs by artists I was into. It was always old music, such as Lucho Gatica, Los Panchos, any sort of Cuban *trova*, Carlos Gardel, Pedro Infante, and José Alfredo Jiménez, rather than what was playing on the radio in those days. I totally isolated myself from the outside world. I didn't listen to the radio, and the only time I turned on the TV was to watch *Los Súper Amigos*, *Gallito Ramírez*, or *Centella*. The rest of the time, I was completely immersed in the records we had around the house, all of which were pop songs. I vaguely recall a couple of Beatles records in the collection, which were perhaps my only reference to mainstream music at that time.

I spent entire days pressing "play" and "stop" on Javier's tape recorder until I finally got what I wanted. The song I played never came out sounding quite the same, but at least it was something similar. I spent hours upon hours listening to music, and little by little, it was becoming an indispensable source of inspiration and pleasure in my life.

■

In class, I was always a good student, if a bit shy and chubby. One of my brothers jokingly called me "toad belly"—man, I wanted to kill him! But hey, what could I expect when all I ever ate was French fries? And when I ate fast food, I always had to order the supersized meals, with mountains of food on the tray. And of course, I had to have my ketchup . . .

I didn't have many friends at school, and focused instead on studying. I wanted to be more fun and outgoing, but my shyness prevented me from doing so. Occasionally, I'd spend recess doing my homework so I could devote my time at home to playing guitar.

My brother Javier sang at school events, and one day, he invited me to accompany him on

guitar and sing backup vocals. We performed well and people enjoyed it. From that moment on, he counted on my participation for every assembly or holiday celebration, but the idea of performing filled me with fear and dread. To this very day, no matter the event, before going onstage, I look up and remind myself that I've been doing this my entire life, that I've seen spotlights and speakers hanging from the ceiling before, that I've known the sounds of the crowd and the smell of smoke, and even still, I feel the exact same nervousness as I did back then. Of course, today I enjoy the process; I'd call it a mixture of pleasure and adrenaline—an absolute addiction to musical expression. A unique way of understanding our passage through this world.

It wasn't easy to go out and sing old music, let alone the same song, when all the girls were crazy about Luis Miguel, the phenomenon at the time. In fact, if memory serves, one of my first conversations with a female classmate was about a Menudo record that she had in her backpack. I barely knew the name of the band, let alone any specific songs or the musical impact they were going to have. She was incredulous—why would I listen to old people's music instead of Luis Miguel? What was I—about thirteen at the time? I can't say, but what I do know is that he had just come on the scene and was already all the rage.

I lived in my own world, lost in thought and yet happy. Carlos Gardel was my idol back then, and my favorite records were by Los

Panchos, Joe Arroyo, and Octavio Mesa. For me, there was no world beyond the pianola in the downstairs cantina of our farmhouse in Carolina del Príncipe or my family's record collections.

I remember thinking acts like Menudo and Luis Miguel were revolutionary in those days. Fever was running rampant: on TV, the radio, the press . . . everyone was talking about them. Fortunately, though, my house was predominantly about Joan Manuel Serrat, Silvio Rodríguez, Francis Cabrel, Cat Stevens, Gardel, and even some Julio Iglesias to balance things out.

■

Even though we lived in a downtown Medellín neighborhood, and between school and home my life was essentially urban, I had a strong connection to the countryside. As far back as I can re-member, we spent every vacation on the farm in Carolina. When the final bell rang on the last day of school, we went straight to the farm. We didn't even stop at home to drop off our books. We spent the next few months there, where everything was fascination and fun, total freedom and safety. And there, I experienced incredible moments that would have a lasting impact upon me.

I'll never forget roaming around the farm with my dad as he bathed or vaccinated livestock. Time slowed down and I felt completely free, enjoying everything from the smell of the fields to even the smell of dried cattle dung and the sweat of the horses.

The farm was about twenty minutes outside Carolina del Príncipe, a little town we always visited on vacations. I always got excited as we approached the farm: you could see the little house in the distance, nestled among mountains separated by a gorge. It was the sort of country cottage typical to Antioquia. Originally, it had only three rooms and a space that could barely be called a kitchen, but with time, we did what we could with what we had to renovate it. The first thing to do was clear a path from the road to the house, which meant we were in for a lot of walking, so everyone—even my sisters—grabbed a shovel or a hoe and got to work. It was a hike, but we all thoroughly enjoyed it.

Once we could get the car to the house, we started remodeling the house itself. To the left was a room my dad used to store horseshoes and saddles, and we converted it into a cantina. My dad wasn't too happy about that. Javier got his hands on a coin-operated pianola, and we all chipped in to help him fashion a wooden bar and some shelving. That little room had a distinct scent of leather and horse sweat that I'll never forget. There, we'd party till dawn, listening to music and singing along. In the other two rooms, we'd sleep if we could, because we were all terrified of the sounds coming down from the mountains just a short distance away. We'd turn off the lights and that's when it all started: talk of ghosts, La Llorona, witches throwing fireballs . . . I

would sweat as if I was in a sauna, but I enjoyed it too much to leave.

We spent our days roaming the most distant pastures to bring the livestock home; we crisscrossed the ravines on foot or horseback, whistling and herding the animals back to the house.

Along with Miguel Hincapié, who was foreman of the estate for many years, we prepared a special bath for the livestock. My brothers and I would stand on the opposite side of the fence to watch the animals jumping around, drenched in *veterana*, which was a liquid my dad used to delouse the animals. We were immediately inundated by that pungent, penetrating smell that today I remember as simply intoxicating. Those were days of absolute glory.

The first thing that I packed for our trips to the farm was my guitar, but if for some reason I forgot mine, my brother had his. Whenever family and friends got together, it was not uncommon for a guitar to emerge so we could strike up songs by Gardel and Los Viscontis, along with a few chords from Octavio Mesa for good measure.

■

It was during my preteen years that I really began to understand the realities of my country. One evening, we were in the car with my sister Mara, who at the time was in her final year of studies at the Instituto Jorge Robledo and with whom I am still very close, and her boyfriend Carlos, driving down Avenida Oriental right in the heart of Medellín. The radio was reporting that members of the M-19 guerrilla group had taken over the Palacio de Justicia in Bogotá and were holding the supreme court hostage. I had no idea what it all meant. Carlos was terrified by the news and tried to explain the severity of the situation and the implications it could have. This was the first conscious image I have of violence in Colombia. My eyes had been opened to a new reality.

In those days, Colombia was locked in a deadly war against both the guerrilla groups and the drug cartels. The country was in a state of upheaval, having tasted the bitterness of corruption and the incurable disease of drug trafficking. Bombings, kidnappings, massacres, the influence of paramilitary groups . . . it was all too much.

Amid this turmoil, and as the years went by, my musical tastes began to spread. Mara's boyfriend Carlos, who also played the guitar, was the one who introduced me to Cuban *trovas*. Silvio Rodríguez, Vicente Feliú, Carlos Varela, Pablo Milanés played more and more frequently on the tape recorders and stereos of my house, and became part of the sound track of my life.

I spent weeks trying to get my guitar to sound like the one Silvio Rodríguez played; in fact, I think the first time I felt something magical about music was when I was trying to re-create his songs. I was twelve years old, and I couldn't even find Cuba on a map. I repeated his lyrics without necessarily taking them to heart—they simply touched my soul. Around the same time that Cuban *trova* entered my life, I was also getting to know the music of Joan Manuel Serrat, Miguel Bosé, Piero, and Nino Bravo, which embodied feelings for high school sweethearts that I could never express, thanks to my own shyness.

In those days, I would just close my eyes and sing right there in my living room. I'd stay up all night practicing and feeling the music in my body and soul. Nothing mattered to me other than playing the guitar, singing, and eating French fries.

For me, a constant reference in my life is the belief that nothing exists without God's will. So every morning and every night I prayed, giving thanks for everything and asking God for His continued blessings for both myself and those people important to me. My world revolved around music, the guitar, the strings, the fingerboard, the tuning pegs, the chords.

It was through the guitar that I found my connection with God and the universe, and it was then that I truly came to understand the meaning of life.

SHOCK

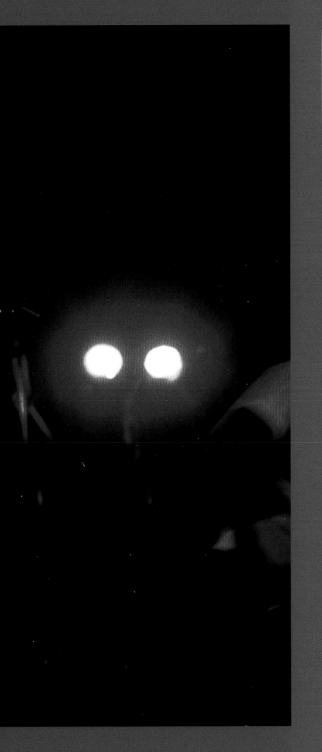

It was in my third year of high school that I first heard the word "rock," and from then on, I spent time between classes with my friends at school, who were also musicians: Caloma, who played a great bass and was in a metal band, perhaps the first quality metal band in all of Medellín; Federico López, a friend whom I respect and remember with great affection and who taught me much about music, the guitar, production, and recording; and Felipe Martínez, who played the drums and would

be a member of Ekhymosis for some time. In those tiny, five-minute sessions, I discovered the bands and the sound that would change me forever: Metallica, Slayer, Iron Maiden, and Kiss.

I'll never forget how I felt when I first heard Metallica's *Kill 'Em All* or Iron Maiden's *The Number of the Beast*. Those albums blew my mind and changed me forever. I was moved by their energy, the speed and aggressiveness of their guitars, the drums, their voices and lyrics, and—despite the fact that I didn't understand a word of English—I connected deeply with the words and music.

I listened to them on old tapes that had been recorded and rerecorded so many times that the sound quality was horrible, but to me it was still the best music on earth! It was pure

romanticism, and it made me want to learn more. I went from listening to pop music straight to metal without so much as a curve in the road. It was a total paradigm shift, as if something inside me had been waiting for this very moment. From here on out, my life was on a new course.

The first few Friday nights I spent out were something completely new to me. I was at once afraid and excited to take on the world. It was then that I began to explore Medellín a bit more. I walked around, I breathed it all in. I was fifteen years old, and those were my first solo excursions into the streets.

Accompanied by Andy—Andrés García, who played bass for Ekhymosis, the group we formed together—I would walk an hour or so from El Poblado park to downtown Medellín with no problem; other times I'd go with Toto, another close friend, from Envigado to El Poblado. I was exploring the city in which I was born and raised, while at the same time com-

ing to terms with my space and the people who inhabited it.

One of my favorite memories is of a house in the Manila neighborhood where they sold Tres Patas wine. It was cheap and would get you seriously drunk. There, we'd gather around for never-ending discussions of music and musicians. What I won't get into is the headaches that came the following day . . .

Medellín was a troubled place in the late 1980s, and life didn't seem to be worth much at all. Rock was what saved and sustained me during those days of violence, fear, frustration, and my own personal shortcomings.

It was on one such Friday that I was wandering from neighborhood to neighborhood looking for a secondhand electric guitar. Life takes such unexpected turns! I'd been saving up for a year to buy an off-road motorcycle, but the moment I discovered rock music, something changed inside of me and all I wanted was an electric guitar. Eventually, in a downtown pawnshop I found an old Cort that I really liked.

With the purchase of that guitar, I left behind the kid who played the acoustic guitar in his living room and found myself face-to-face with my city and my destiny while learning how to play the electric guitar. It was around that time that Andy and I formed Ekhymosis.

I was young and full of energy, and I wanted to take on the world. Andrés was studying electrical engineering, which was ex-

actly how I met him: he'd come over to patch up that first electric guitar, and I happened to ask if he could teach me how to play with a pick.

We got the name "Ekhymosis" from a medical book we found in the house of our drummer, Esteban Mora. We were looking for a term that sounded strange and very hard to pronounce. We ended up liking "ecchymosis," the medical term for a bruise or swelling of the skin caused by impact.

By the time I started playing with Ekhymosis, the violence in Colombia—and especially in Medellín—was in full swing. The drug cartels had publically declared war on the police, the military, and the establishment at large. Colombia was in a constant state of threat; bombs were exploding every night, and people were being murdered in droves. Clearly, all this affected the way we thought, composed music, and lived in that city.

We painted our canvas with brusque strokes. Even if we wanted to create a butterfly, it was impossible to ignore the patently hostile environment in which we lived. In our lyrics, we sang about what we didn't understand, we asked questions, we vented our pain and frustration. Slowly but surely, music was becoming at once a powerful means of expression and a means of escape. We clung to it as if our lives depended on it, and we gave it everything we had, back then and still today.

One night, I went with several friends from school out to Casa Verde, a bar in an old co-

lonial house located atop one of the many hills that dotted the El Poblado neighborhood. We sat down, placed our orders, and when the waiter returned to our table with the drinks, he suddenly said, his voice on high alert, "Get out of here—go home as fast as you can . . . There was a mass murder at another bar just around the corner."

Terrified and confused, we all ran home. A couple hours later, the news broke on radio, TV, and the papers, such that the entire country bore witness to that macabre night I'll never forget. The lead read: On June 29, 1990, several armed men disguised as police entered the Oporto Bar shouting threats. They forced the patrons to lie facedown on the floor before shooting them point-blank in the head.

That night, nineteen people were mercilessly killed. Nineteen kids were gunned down in cold blood. Among them was a young man named Camilo, a friend from school we'd affectionately nicknamed Conavi. I'd even given him some guitar lessons.

I woke up the next day hoping the events of the previous night were just a dream—a nightmare. The whole country was stunned by such a barbaric act, and I still couldn't believe it was true. I picked up the phone and dialed Camilo's number. Just as I had, Camilo had gone to a bar the night before to spend some time with friends. And now he was dead. I just couldn't bring myself to

EKTHYMOSIS

NUNCA
NADA
NUEVO...
DEMO-88

believe it. I felt in my heart that if I called him he'd answer the phone and everything would be okay. The housekeeper picked up on the other end. "Hey, could you pass the phone to Camilo, please?" She replied, sobbing, "No, Juan . . . Camilo's dead. They killed him last night in Oporto." And that's when I finally came to terms with the fact that my friend was dead and that this nightmare was very real.

Oporto was one of the many massacres we endured in Medellín and in Colombia during the worst years of terrorism. I just couldn't understand what was happening to my city and my country. Over time I learned how to process it, but back then nothing that was happening made any sense. Life wasn't worth anything and fear was everywhere.

The enormity of the violence and the frustration of those days only drove my passion for metal to even greater heights. The simple act of listening to distorted guitar riffs along with battering drums made me feel free and relaxed. It was a way of releasing all the feelings of rage and pain that had begun to take over my soul. I learned how to headbang with my long, flowing mane . . . and I heard a group that would come to have a big impact on me.

The first time I listened to *Reign in Blood* by Slayer, I was sitting in my dad's car in the garage, tuning in to a metal program that came on the radio every night at ten. When the show was over, I put in a borrowed tape, cranked the volume up to ten, and I almost died—I literally almost died! I couldn't believe it: the guitars, the speed, the aggression—it all blew my mind. I'd never be the same.

Later, I heard *Kill 'Em All* by Metallica, and that pretty much sealed the deal: everything had changed. It was one of those rare moments in life where you can catch a glimpse of your future. In the deepest reaches of my being, I suddenly understood one thing: music is my destiny. There, in the middle of a

ON YOUR KNEES

The premier colombian speed metal band is back with their new 12"EP "DE RODILLAS". 4 down to earth tracks of intense melodic speed featurig "NO ES JUSTO" & "SALVAME". This EP should find a place in your music collection.

TO ORDER: Send US$ 10.00 (postage included)
To: STIGMA PRODUCCIONES
A.A. 55412
Medellin, COLOMBIA
South America

STIGMA
PRODUCCOONES

violent Medellín, I had found an impenetrable refuge in music. Music showed me the way to defeat fear and timidity and vent out the rage I felt inside about this city in chaos, this city at war.

My interest in music was growing by leaps and bounds, and the country's situation was gradually taking its toll on my reality. Kidnappings, massacres, guerrilla soldiers, narco gangsters . . . so many words that were never part of my vocabulary before were now normal, everyday words like "bread" or "milk."

Every day, the news reported more and more lurid acts of violence, sinking the nation deeper and deeper into tragedy.

One unforgettable day, that tragedy knocked on our door.

The victim, my cousin José Alejandro Aristizabal, was the youngest of ten siblings. After studying in Brazil, he'd returned to Colombia, and his work as a veterinarian in the small town of Frontino, in western Antioquia, required him to spend a lot of time on the road. One damned day, the guerrillas took him. His family only received news of the kidnapping from a local farmer, and they didn't learn anything else for some time. Emperatriz, his mom, and Emiro, his dad—my own father's brother—said that every time the doorbell rang, they ran to the door, thinking he had finally come home.

After five long, agonizing months, the family finally received news about José Alejandro's fate: a ransom note for twenty-five million pesos.

Somehow, Emperatriz and Emiro managed to scrounge up the money. They contacted the officials to set up the exchange. Only then did they learn that their son was already dead. The

twenty-five million was for the return of his body, and the only way to reach the location was by plane.

   Although he had been buried for over five months, they found his body battered and beaten but mostly intact. Because he had been buried at high altitude in a very cold region, decomposition was minimal and there was little odor. The death of José Alejandro was a deep wound to our entire family, evidence of the reality of the country in which we were living. He was thirty-seven years old.

In those days, Ekhymosis became my greatest outlet. My life, my dreams, my time . . . everything revolved around the band. We rehearsed every day and every night. The band was our sickness, our obsession, our vice, our addiction. On the day that my aunt Pastora died, I was trying to play Metallica's "Fade to Black" by ear with my acoustic guitar.

It felt as if I were living outside of reality, such was the anesthetizing power of music: however sad I felt, I also felt joy because music had entered my life in such a transformative way. Playing guitar, rehearsing with the band, and working on my music became the only way I could live in the face of such pain and such unimaginable violence. It became my form of healing.

3

SEARCHING

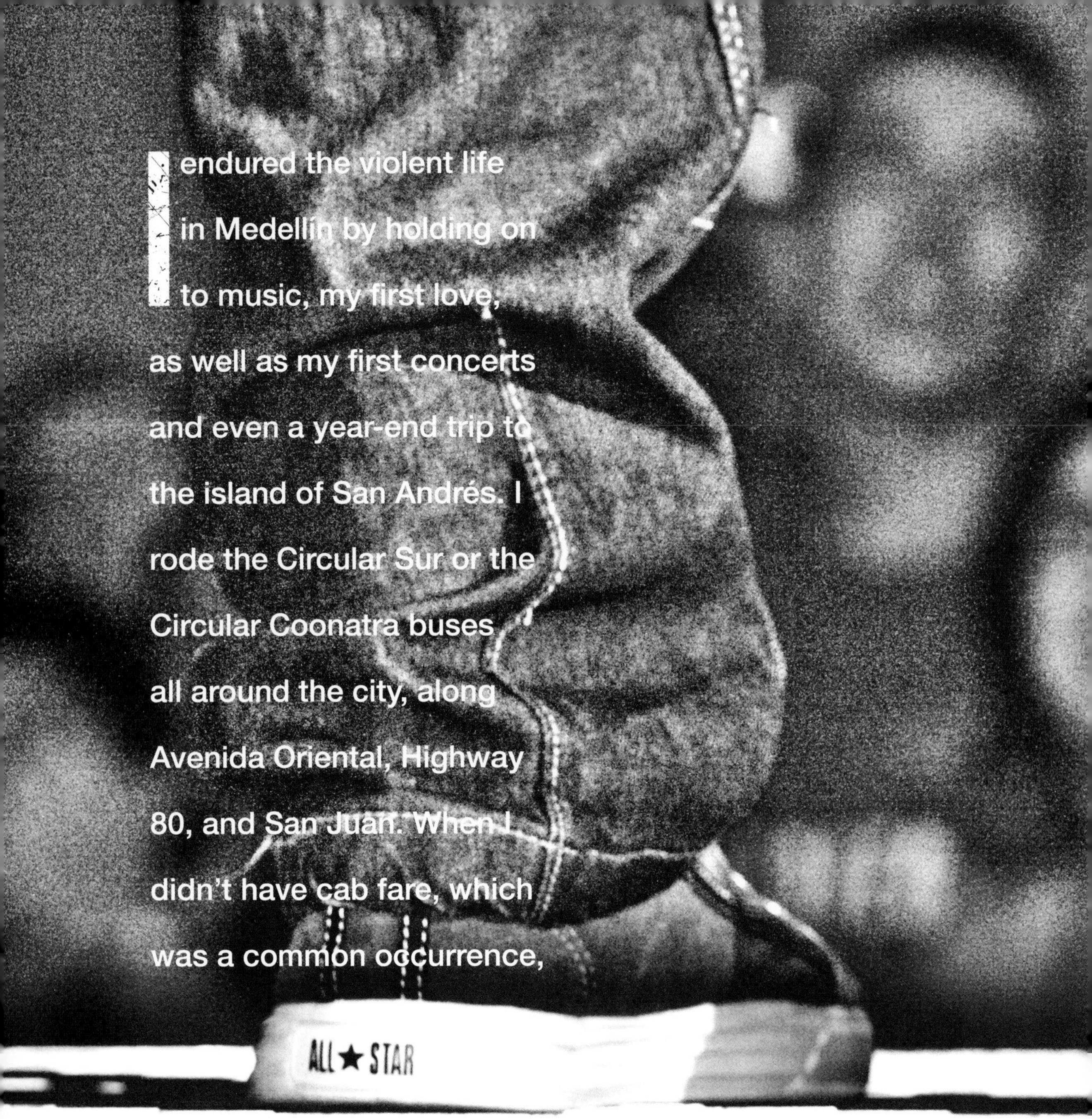

I endured the violent life
in Medellín by holding on
to music, my first love,
as well as my first concerts
and even a year-end trip to
the island of San Andrés. I
rode the Circular Sur or the
Circular Coonatra buses
all around the city, along
Avenida Oriental, Highway
80, and San Juan. When I
didn't have cab fare, which
was a common occurrence,

I'd hop a bus with my guitar slung over my shoulder and an amp in my hand in order to get to rehearsal, which took place in a studio in the home of the famous Luis Emilio and was the only place that metal bands could jam until all hours of the night. It was basically a tiny room with a few spare instruments.

My love for metal was as strong as the love I had for my other musical roots, the more traditional music I inherited from my father and brothers. But my first foray was as blinding as it was radical. I completely abandoned the acoustic guitar in order to dedicate myself to studying and playing every song by Metallica, Led Zeppelin, and others.

After everything I'd lived, saw, heard, and felt during the day, I would come home at night, lie down on my bed, close my eyes, and pray. I connected with God in a very personal way that's all but impossible to describe. It was my moment of insight and reflection, a state of mind that is at once simple and profound. That special moment when unplugging yourself from the physical world leads to a connection with immaterial things in a flash of searching and meditation. Those moments of abstraction have always been a part of my life, no matter what music accompanies them.

■

My room was covered with posters of James Hetfield, Metallica, the Beatles, Kerry King,

Slayer, and Kreator. I'd even painted the logo of the German thrash band Destruction on my wall. Metal was all anyone was talking about, so I did my homework, listening carefully to different bands to find the ones I enjoyed the most and the ones with which I identified in some way, shape, or form. This kind of music never got much airplay on the radio or TV. Back then, it was basically an underground movement. We had to make do with pirated copies and bootlegs; only people with money could afford to buy the original, so the rest of us would have to dub it.

One afternoon, I was working on a poster for a social studies class when my brother José walked in to find me blasting *The Number of the Beast* by Iron Maiden at full volume. To be honest, I couldn't understand a single word in the entire song, but I still felt completely drawn to it—it was a pure connection with the music and energy. Seeing me like that, my brother left the room and went straight to my mom to inform her that she needed to pay more attention to me.

That began my rebellious phase: I wore my hair long, I fought to go against the flow of the establishment, and I looked for a way—any way at all—to be different. In high school, I fought against the standard rule of short hair for boys and had to suffer the consequences until I reached college and finally had the freedom to really grow my hair long.

Music was my refuge and my way of connecting with the universe. I'd spend entire days play-

ing guitar, singing in front of the mirror, and listening to songs that moved me. Ekhymosis awakened in me all sorts of dreams and fantasies and represented the beginning of what my life has been ever since. I usually composed songs with Andy, but I'd often arrive at rehearsal with an idea that we'd all share.

In March of 1988, we had our first major gig, held at the sports complex in the city of Envigado. That night, I remember sitting in the stands behind the stage with the rest of the band: Esteban Mora, drums; Andy, guitar; and Alex Oquendo, vocals. We waited anxiously for our turn. When the time came, the concert promoter walked up to us and said, "Guys, get out there—you're on." And at that exact moment, I froze. I don't have a single memory of what happened next . . . only photos can help me prove to myself that I actually was on that stage that night. Thanks to my stage fright, I forgot everything, but the band rocked.

The place wasn't packed, but it wasn't empty either. I'd say there were around two thousand people. At the time, I just played guitar, as did Andy, while Alex sang vocals with Esteban on drums. We didn't have a bassist, nor did we even realize what we were missing. We ripped through our set without following the playlist, running on pure heart and adrenaline. It was all about dis-

covery: we were eager to see ourselves as musicians, as good people living in a violent city. We were bursting with life and peace. Ever since then, music has been my salvation. It's the way I commune with life itself.

We gradually got to know people on the local scene—musicians, artists, and engineers—who were working with the same enthusiasm as we were. A year after our first concert, we were more established on the scene and looking to record a better demo.

If I remember correctly, we were sitting in the basement of Federico López's house—the man who would later become Ekhymosis's sound engineer and whom I will never forget for being a mentor, teacher, and adviser to many musicians, including myself—when we asked him to record a five-track demo tape for us. Playing fast and hard was our only objective, but we needed something else, since we weren't exactly the best musicians.

On Friday afternoons after class, I'd stop by Federico's house to watch the rehearsals of Ekrion, a favorite local metal band. They were totally underground. Only people who were truly into metal knew about them, but they were, without a doubt, some of the best musicians I've seen. As I watched El Gato on drums, Jorge on lead guitar, and Federico on rhythm guitar, I'd say to myself, *Wow. One day I'd like to be able to play like those dudes.*

We always surrounded ourselves with inspiration: the great bands like Sepultura, Metallica,

Slayer, Anthrax, and Kreator, as well as the bad reviews that motivated us to rehearse even more. We wanted to be the best metal band out there, and for years, we didn't miss a single day of rehearsal. We made the demo to start publicizing the band and also to exercise our chops in the recording studio. I still have the case to that original demo.

■

The first time Ekhymosis played outside of Medellín was in March of 1988. I remember it like it was yesterday. The phone in the house rang, and when I picked it up, I heard this on the other end of the line:

"Hey, Juanes, how you been, bro? My name's Hueso. I wanna invite you guys to come play a concert in Pereira. The only thing is, you gotta pay for everything."

I almost shouted my response:

"Hell yeah, bro—of course! Just tell me what we gotta do!"

Pereira is a separate city from Medellín. This would be the first time I really got out of my familial bubble.

Before heading out for Pereira, we decided to meet up at my house because it was the most central location. There was Esteban with some music stands, Andy with his custom-built guitar (which had more spikes than curves, though marvelous nonetheless), and me with the rest of our guitars slung over my shoulder. We walked down El Palo until we hit La Oriental. There, we waited for a bus that would take us to the central terminal, where we could catch another bus to Pereira.

That trip was pure joy. We were the only three people on the bus, sitting in the back row of seats and drinking beer, feeling as if we were on the most luxurious private jet. The trip lasted all night long, and we arrived at dawn the next day. I hadn't met Hueso, the promoter, in person, so it was great to meet him there at the terminal.

From the terminal, we went straight to the hotel. We were exhausted and couldn't wait to lie down and nap for a while. As we pulled up, we noticed that the place wasn't as nice as we'd expected. It wasn't even a hotel—it was more of a dingy motel. But the excitement we felt at being in a new city, getting ready to perform in front of a completely different audience, was all that mattered. When we entered our room, I lay down on the bed and, much to my surprise, discovered that there was a giant mirror on the ceiling directly above the bed. I wondered, why

would anyone put a mirror—? Heh heh . . . then I got it!

When it came time for us to be introduced and step out onstage, I was terrified standing there in front of a mob of metalheads who didn't know a single note to any of our songs. Since this was our first non-local show, we didn't have a sound engineer or tech. We played five songs, and it was like we were back in the days of the Beatles. There was barely any amplification, and the crowd couldn't hear a thing. I didn't speak so much as a word between songs, I didn't move around the stage, and I had to force myself to blink and breathe. It was a near fatal case of stage fright. The crowd started throwing pieces of brick and tile at us. Something bad had happened, but we couldn't tell what it was. We had no idea whether it was because of us or because they couldn't hear anything . . . It was as terrifying as it was marvelous. Only later did we learn that the problem wasn't with the sound, but that a very popular band had canceled at the last minute.

Ultimately, we couldn't care less about what happened that night or how the concert ended . . . We felt triumphant! We'd left Medellín and were on our way to conquering the world!

■

A number of years went by. The band grew stronger, the studio sessions changed, and we played other cities with better results. We even returned to Pereira on a number of occasions, and it became something of a common denominator for our activities and meetings. Band members came and went. We were in full experimental mode and in full search for identity. What started out as a metal band was transformed into a laboratory, though not everyone agreed on the philosophy.

Eventually, the band recorded its first EP with Víctor García, himself a great musician from Medellín who also had the best recording studio at the time. Since we still didn't have a record deal or anyone backing us, we had to pay for recording and producing the album out of our own pockets. We scraped together some money and recorded four tracks, which we then sold to family, friends, and fans.

Word was getting out about the band, and with it came new people with new ideas, proposals, and concerts. All our dedication and work was finally beginning to bear fruit, and after five years in the game we could say that the band was ready to take the next step. Finally, miraculously, we got the call we'd all been hoping for: Codiscos, a small record label specializing in *vallenato* music and headed by the dear Dr. Álvaro Arango, was the first company to believe in us. I felt like the sky was the limit, that everything was coming together, that this was our next great challenge and opportunity to grow even bigger in Colombia.

We signed a contract with Codiscos to record our first LP. It was total joy. A dream. We

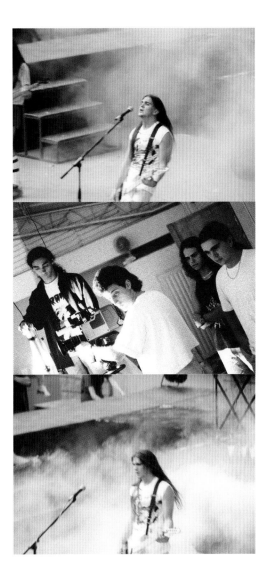

couldn't believe it. We rehearsed constantly and wherever we could—rather, wherever people could stand our deafening racket. Sometimes we rehearsed at Esteban's farm in La Estrella, on the patio behind my house, or in Andy's living room, but in the end we always managed to find someone who would put up with our music. We forgot all about the outside world; nothing existed beyond Ekhymosis.

After all the rehearsals, we finally recorded the album at Tita Maya's studio on the top floor of the Carlos E. Restrepo building, with Federico López as our sound engineer and producer. Every morning, I woke up with an ear-to-ear smile on my face because I knew I'd be spending the entire day in the studio. I walked from my house to Avenida Oriental, where I caught a Circular Coonatra bus that would drop me off right at the studio. I walked up the five flights of stairs and joined the rest of the team there. Everyone was excited, full of life, and ready to record. We put a lot of hard work into our first LP, which we ended up titling *Niño Gigante* and was scheduled to hit stores in 1993. Up until then, we'd had only a four-track and a two-track EP to our name.

For the album's release, we needed photos, and for that we contacted Andrés Sierra to set up a photo shoot for the band. We picked out one shot that we all liked for the album cover, but (as usual) the label didn't agree. So Andrés hit the streets and somehow got a picture of a kid pointing a handgun right at the camera lens. We loved it—even more than the other shots. We were just

crazy about this black-and-white that perfectly caught the force and rage of our songs and the angry, aggressive lyrics we had written. And this photo still exists today.

We showed the photo to Dr. Arango. His verdict—as we all expected—was negative. He explained that the studio wasn't willing to take any media criticism that would inevitably come from such a stark image, especially considering the violent state of the city at that time. We were disappointed but not disillusioned, and as is often the case in these sorts of situations, we had to accept it. In the end, the photo we used for the album cover was much more conceptual.

The album was released in 1993 to positive

reviews, and to promote it we played relent-lessly every weekend.

Finally it was out. That moment is recorded in my memory like my First Communion. I ran around the house like a lunatic, and my mom ran after me, wondering what had happened. I was screaming. We'd fulfilled a nearly im-possible dream: in an era dominated by pop and techno music, we'd been granted a space for our own, unique sound.

In some cities, the radio would play the only ballad on the album: "Solo." We had an agreement between friends and family mem-bers to call and request the song on the radio.

I called dozens of times myself, changing my voice so they wouldn't recognize me . . . Thank God we didn't have today's technology back then, or else they would have caught me red-handed!

Andy and I had written the lyrics for "Solo" on a bus from Medellín to Cali. We'd come up with the music during our rehearsals, and right from the start we felt like we had something

special with this song. From the moment it first hit the airwaves, it made an impact, slowly climbing the charts, and by the end of the year it had become the number one song in the country and the most requested song on rock radio.

Niño Gigante is, in my opinion, the best album we produced as a band during our twelve years, on par with the final one, the green album, which was released in 1997.

■

The Ekhymosis years had it all: love, heartbreak, critics, depression, joy, parties, bombs, kidnappings, news, college, and my bike.

In college, I reconnected with Miote, an old friend from high school days. Along with two others—Nico and Pájaro—we went one day to a neighborhood in Antioquia to pick up two cardboard boxes containing one of the great loves of my life: my first motorcycle, a 1972 KZ 1000 custom.

Andrés, another friend from high school, had a small garage, and there I patiently assembled my beautiful burnt orange baby. All the money I'd earned from Ekhymosis went into that bike: pistons, rings, tires, hydraulics, bolts, screws, headlights, wiring, oil, gas, chrome, and thousands and thousands of other details.

College continued. I started studying mechanical engineering at Escuela de Administración, Finanzas y Tecnología, and after a semester of hell, I transferred to Universidad

Pontificia Bolivariana, where I started studying advertising. The next semester I switched to industrial design, which was the program I eventually completed. In class, I was thinking about rehearsals; during phys ed, my mind was on guitars; and during my commute on the bus or metro (since my motorcycle wasn't quite fixed up yet), I had lyrics and melodies running through my mind.

I had nightmares about the bike and about concerts: that the engine wouldn't start, that nobody would show up. These continued until the motorcycle was finished, and fortunately the shows always drew a crowd—some larger than others—but there were always at least a few people who came out to listen to us.

The day I got the bike, I just couldn't believe it. I rode all around the city like a madman set free. Although it was fresh out of the garage, it was still a classic 1972 bike, and you could see me coming from a mile away with the sound of the muffler, the gaudy color, and the trail of smoke I left behind me, since the pistons and rings weren't quite up to par. But it ran, a thousand cc's of brute strength. I loved that animal for many years, and it became my favorite means of transportation.

It got me to rehearsal, to class; I punched the clock, went for a ride, and much more. It was part of my life, and I was lucky enough to never wreck it—several hundred pounds of steel crashing down on your legs would have been a pretty painful thing.

■

My dad loved living in downtown Medellín. Because everything was within walking distance, he didn't have to drive, catch the bus, or take a taxi. My mom followed in his footsteps, and from the two of them, I caught the bug as well. During my teenage years and college days, I understood the importance of being in the heart of the city, listening to all sorts of sounds: the street vendors, the cars, the waves of people walking this way and that.

During the week, my dad would walk a few blocks to the intersection of La Playa and La Oriental to see a few friends. It was easy for him to run errands to the banks and hardware stores where he bought the supplies before sending them to his convenience store at the edge of the Carolina del Príncipe plaza. He used to leave in his car on Monday around noon to drive the unpaved roads to Carolina. Later, he decided not to drive anymore, so I began taking him there, though sometimes it was one of my brothers—Jaime, José, or Javier—who accompanied him.

For me, those car trips were some of the most special moments I ever shared with my dad. We had three hours to talk about anything and everything, plus the time we had in Carolina. My father

was a fairly reserved man who didn't talk much, but he always asked me about my music, about the band, and he insisted that I finish my studies. That was a constant theme during our discussions, and he was right about it. Ten years after he passed away, I received my degree from Universidad Pontificia Bolivariana.

Once we reached Carolina del Príncipe, my dad would spend the whole day at the store until closing time, around nine at night, when he'd meet up with some friends at a corner of the park to chat. I'd see him from afar, with his poncho and hat, always very serious and proper. Then we'd walk to the house together, and as we opened the door, my heart would start beating faster. It was a beautiful ranch-style house common in Antioquia, with a long hallway leading to a central courtyard and the surrounding rooms. By this time, the only remaining members of that side of the family were my father and my aunt Marta; the others had passed away in the previous five years and we'd kept a vigil over them in one of the adjoining rooms, as is the custom.

I slept in a bed near his. I'll never forget how when the lights were turned off, I couldn't see anything at all. It was absolute darkness. I'd wave my hands directly in front of my face, but it was useless. Zero visibility. And the only sound you could hear was the occasional rat skittering across the bedroom ceiling.

The only way to kill the deathly silence of Carolina nights was for my dad to flip on the shortwave radio that could pick up signals from other countries in other languages, stuff we could barely even understand. My dad just did it so we wouldn't have to listen to the silence.

When my college coursework and the band's touring and concert schedule intensified, my dad decided it would be better if I didn't go with him to Carolina anymore. He starting making the trip by bus. At the time, I didn't understand his decision, and now, looking back on it, it makes me sad that I didn't get to accompany him more.

Though the mode of transportation had changed, the routine was the same: he'd board the first bus bound for Carolina with his poncho, his hat, and his empty milk canister. Invariably, that canister would return a few days later brimming with milk fresh from the cow along with a package of meat and that oozing kind of cheese that I hated. At home we always had milk, cheese, and meat from Carolina del Príncipe; it was one of the constants in my life and didn't change until many years later.

A week before my father died, Dad and I drove up Avenida El Poblado to my sister Luz's house. I was behind the wheel of the blue 1953 Chevy that my brother occasionally loaned me to get to class or for going out on the weekends. My dad was upset about my long hair—he was, ultimately, more conservative than my mom—and we were discussing the issue. Suddenly I said, rather sharply, "Look—I'm not gonna chop my hair off, so just drop it."

I never imagined that a week later he'd be lying in a hospital, near death. For years, I'd regret arguing with him over something as stupid as that.

My father's death was sudden and unexpected. My brother Jaime called us at home one day to tell us that, after an operation that seemed to have gone perfectly well, Dad had taken a turn for the worse. My mom and I rushed to his side. I convinced myself that it wasn't serious and that he'd be fine—that's what I was telling my mom the whole way to the clinic, trying to be calming and supportive.

When we got there, we saw that the door to his room was ajar. From the hallway, I could see my dad lying there, surrounded by doctors, nurses, cables, and equipment. I was in shock. I immediately turned away so I wouldn't have to see any more. I stood there outside the room with one of my brothers, and as I looked down the hall I saw a priest dressed in a cassock walking toward us, almost in slow motion, carrying a Bible and holy water. The moment he entered the room, I knew my father was dying.

I remember when my mom threw open my bedroom door and said, "Wake up, Juan. Your father has died." My God, what an awful moment in time.

It's been almost twenty years since my father died. My relationship with God and the spiritual connection with my father get stronger each and every day. Although I can't see him, I know he's been with me all these years and that he's watching over me and caring for me the way I now do with my own children. I talk to him constantly in my prayers, I ask God to bless his soul with happiness, and I believe with absolute certainty that he's at peace now, somewhere in the universe, or in all places at once.

■

Between 1997 and 1998, Ekhymosis — the band I'd been with for nearly twelve years — came to an end. Fatigue and creative differences were gradually bringing us to what amounted to death by natural causes. It was a hard blow to take. I felt as though I'd lost everything, that my dreams of being an artist and musician had ended. I was completely disillusioned, deceived, and frustrated, but it was a time when — yet again — music was able to save me. My feelings of depression were never as strong as my true love for music. So to put an end to that phase of my life and to move on with passion, I decided to look toward other horizons.

I wanted my next step to take me to the United States.

■

Although several years passed between the end of Ekhymosis and the beginning of my solo career, I recorded a few demos on my computer with a program called Cakewalk. At the same time, I was planning my trip to the United States. The first thing I did was sell my

stuff: my bike, my amps, my computer, and a few other things. It was hard leaving so much behind, but I couldn't see any alternatives. My faith in God and in what my inner voice was telling me was so strong that all I could do was follow. I knew what I had to do.

In 1997, I had everything solidified, and I bought an American Airlines ticket to Miami with a stopover in Bogotá, because there were no direct flights from Medellín to the United States. I had a window seat overlooking one of the wings. I watched the other passengers boarding the plane, and among them was a big Colombian rock band, Aterciopelados, on their way to the Grammys. I thought to myself, *My God, what am I doing? Give me the strength to go on . . .*

I landed in Miami with big hopes and little money. Just my guitar and an orange backpack full of CDs and a couple of books and documents. For the first few months, I crashed with Memo, a great buddy whose taste in metal was very similar to my own. Days passed and I dreamed, composed, walked, ran, slept, and occasionally helped him with his graphic design work. I'd roam the streets like a madman, going to whatever concerts I could, to the movies, the bookstore, wherever.

I slept on the carpet and covered myself with a blanket that another friend of ours had lent me.

Time didn't exist for me; it was as if I'd steeled myself against suffering, living in the moment and protected by my faith in God alone.

Every day I'd go for a run for about thirty or forty minutes, during which time I'd pray and meditate. I drew mental pictures of what I wanted my future to look like: onstage singing, rehearsing in a studio, or signing a record contract. I spent only three months in Miami because I felt that the city's music vibe wasn't quite what I was looking for. Miami had a different sound back then. My dream had always been to work with Gustavo Santaolalla. He lived in Los Angeles, so getting to the City of Angels became my new objective.

But first, I made a stop in New York. I had a friend in the music industry, and he lent me an apartment. I spent two months just walking: I'd leave in the morning and return to the apartment at night so exhausted that all I could do was sleep. The feeling of waking up in the morning and not having any idea what would come of my life filled me with terror and fear, but at the same time I was able to connect more with my dad and with God. I prayed and rested. More than once, I found myself tearing up, filled with feelings of loneliness and desperation, starting from scratch in an unknown country whose language I couldn't even speak.

New York was too much for me at the time, since I didn't have any money and had very few contacts there, and so that's when I decided to finally make the move to Los Angeles, where I knew of a couple of people who might be able to help me out. When the plane landed, I grabbed my bags, exited the airport, and knew instinctively that I was in my element. I knew I'd be breathing this air for many years to come. I felt an immediate connection to the city. I had the support of great friends, true angels who offered me a helping hand during that time of aimlessness, hours

and hours riding on buses, composing, reading in bookstores, and sending out demos to anyone who would listen.

I was hoping to get a record deal. Time passed, and both my money and my patience were running thin. I kept my cash in a little pocket of my reversible green and orange bomber jacket—it was my mobile bank. Whenever I started feeling anxious, I'd stick my hand in that pocket to reassure myself that I still had enough left to eat.

I spent my days downtown, or in Wilshire, Pasadena, Glendale, Griffith Park . . . wherever I could find a place to sleep or eat. I still didn't have a record deal, but I was adamant: don't go home without achieving your dream.

The three years or so that I spent in the United States pursuing my dream were full of learning, reflection, and above all connection . . . both with God and with myself. I gave up everything in Medellín in order to start anew. There were times when all I had was rice to eat and tap water to drink, since I didn't have money for anything else.

During one of my many moves, I found a motel in Beverly Hills for two hundred dollars a week. It was strange to find myself in a tiny motel room on such a prestigious area, lined with luxurious condos and houses. I'd spend most of the day in that room with the curtains closed, playing and singing and recording what I wrote on my little Tascam four-track cassette recorder.

The phone in the motel room was red, like the one in the Batman movies. One afternoon when I came back from a walk—something I did every day to help stay focused—it rang. I ran to answer it because, in all the time I was there, nobody had ever called me.

It was the voice of Marusa Reyes and the famous producer Gustavo Santaolalla. I couldn't believe it! I was so emotional that I could have burst into tears. They said they wanted to sign me to their Surco label, a Universal division managed by Santaolalla. From that moment, I felt neither the uncertainty of whether all my hard work would pay off nor the stress of facing the difficult challenges ahead. I felt only the sense that the sacrifice had been well worth the pain, that God had heard me and that my dad had helped.

I met with Gustavo, Marusa, and Aníbal Kerpel, one of their associates, at a café on Sunset. I began a new life.

Two weeks later, I had the most enjoyable recording session ever. I emerged and spent the rest of the day at La Casa—Gustavo and Aníbal's studio—working, recording, moving things around, chatting, and learning. My first solo album, *Fíjate Bien*, was finished in late 1999 in LA with Gustavo, Aníbal, and myself as producers.

By the time the record was finished, I had spent two full years in LA and my desire to return to Colombia was overwhelming. I needed to go home, hug my family, sleep in my old bed with my pillow and blankets, and eat my mom's food. I booked a flight with a layover of a couple days in

Miami. It was then that I realized everything was changing. Now that I had a record deal and an album under my belt, I didn't feel the anxiety I'd felt a few years before, when I first set foot in that city. I was happy and at peace with the knowledge that I was living my dream and that nothing in the world could tear it away from me.

That brief stay in Miami was quite productive as well, since I was able to meet Manolo Díaz, president of Universal, who helped me through the process of finalizing the contract and who also introduced me to the man who would become my manager for the next decade.

And so it was that, after a two-year absence, I returned to Medellín in late 1999, just in time for the holidays.

I embraced my mom for what seemed like an hour. I just couldn't let go. I also reconnected with my siblings, my friends, and the rest of the family. I felt so happy to be among so many people and so much love, especially considering everything that had happened in the past few years. But it had all been worth it.

GLORY

4

Incredible times followed. I went from radio station to radio station, visiting every corner of Latin America, singing and playing guitar to promote the album. I went all over the Spanish-speaking world: Puerto Rico, the United States, Central America, South America, and Spain. It was often difficult for my music to find the right place on the airwaves, because some felt that it was too pop for the more rock stations, and too

rock for the pop stations. But we started to connect with people, and that never let up. Word of mouth gradually increased, and with the work being done by both the record label's management team and by myself, good things were coming our way.

It wasn't easy, and we didn't sell many CDs, but when the 2001 Latin Grammys came around, *Fíjate Bien* had gotten seven nominations.

The day the invitation to the Latin Grammys arrived, I was participating in a telethon in Guatemala. At first, I didn't want to go, but my colleagues convinced me otherwise, and a few days later I was boarding a plane for Miami. There, I stayed at the home of Andrés Recio, who worked for the management team.

My Nike sneakers were still wet from washing them the day before for press conferences, so I set them in a window to dry overnight, and then I stuck them behind the fridge up against the fan. But none of these home remedies worked—when I put them on, they were still damp and cold. I laughed it off and said to Andrés, "Hey, man, there's nothing we can do. Let's just go!"

That afternoon, they read my name seven times, once for each nomination. It was my first chance to see other famous artists, and I felt as if I were walking on air. I just couldn't grasp what

was happening: seven nominations for a debut album was almost unheard of.

One headline read, "Juanes, the Perfect Stranger." After that came the whirlwind of interviews, trips, and more trips, because we'd been invited to join the Watcha Tour and play all across Latin America and the United States. Everything was pure joy.

There were a couple of months between the announcement of the nominees and the ceremony itself, during which we did a tireless run of interviews and video shoots: one in Canada for "Fíjate Bien" and one for "Podemos Hacernos Daño" in Bogotá. While we were filming the latter of these two videos,

something special happened—something very special indeed. One of the models for the shoot was Karen Martínez, the actress and former beauty queen from Cartagena.

And that's where the love of my life began.

It was true love, a relationship that evolved to become the center of my existence. We fell madly in love with each other the first moment we met, and we promised ourselves it would last forever. And that's how we came to live together in a small apartment in Bogotá that she paid for, since I didn't yet have the means to do so. During those first few months with Karen, I had to travel for concerts, promotion, and so forth. Meanwhile, she had to stay in Colombia for work, meaning we had to spend the majority of our time apart.

From the very beginning of our relationship, distance was the hurdle we had to overcome—as it still would be even years later—but we were devoted to each other.

With *Fíjate Bien*, I had given shape to my dark side, but now with Karen I had discovered the light of my life. When I had saved up a bit more money, we moved to another small apartment in Bogotá and it was there that I composed almost all of my second album, *Un Día Normal*.

My energy was different. I was more optimistic than ever, I'd survived those trying years, and now I felt strong and ready to continue. I didn't have a studio per se, so I took advantage of Karen's sound equipment and connected it to my computer. From that creative phase, in that little room decorated with posters of Bob Marley, Elvis Presley, and Jimi Hendrix, came songs like "Es Por Ti," "A Dios Le Pido," "La Paga," and "Fotografía."

Amid all the traveling, changes, and days of absolute joy, the date for the Latin Grammys was fast approaching: September 11, 2001. The event was to take place in LA, and I flew there with Karen, my mother, my cousin, and my sister. It was a dream . . . I couldn't believe that

two years after having lived in that city, enduring some of the most solitary and difficult times of my life, I was preparing for music's most important night. We reached our hotel, and the whole world was there, from artists to journalists, and while it was all a bit crazy, the positive energy was palpable.

After the trip, I was so tired and stressed that I could barely speak. I went to my room to take a nap, but not before spending a moment with my mother and sister to thank God for the life we were living.

The next morning I awoke to a phone call. It was seven thirty in the morning and my manager

was on the other end of the line telling me to turn on CNN, that something had happened in New York. I turned on the TV to see the unforgettably terrifying images that, to this day, still make me cringe.

On the screen I could see the World Trade Center tower aflame and a mountain of smoke billowing out of a gigantic hole in the side of the building. We still didn't know exactly what had happened, and I remember the reporter was choked with emotion, barely able to speak. Karen and I sat there paralyzed, speechless.

Minutes later, we saw the second plane hit the other tower. "Oh, my God," we said to ourselves. "What's happening?" It was the most bone-chilling thing I had ever seen. The place I'd always dreamed of as being safe was now the target of terrorism, and with these attacks, the whole world was as well.

The anchor was giving information about survivors and fire-

fighters, and there was speculation about war, an accident,

and terrorism. Suddenly, the first tower began to collapse. The

anchor was struck silent for a moment before being able to

say, simply, "My God." Minutes later, the second tower went

down, and the world changed forever.

I was worried: any of my friends or family members—or even myself—could have been on one of those planes. I wondered what the victims would have felt just before death, and what their families would have been feeling at that moment. I don't think the human mind can fully comprehend the horror that occurred on that day. My deep feelings of pain for what had transpired in New York were tinged with sadness, because the wonderful night that we had all been planning and waiting for had been destroyed.

I said to my mother, my voice all but a whisper in the face of such tragedy: "Life is so ironic, Mom. Today was supposed to be the most important day of my life, and now it's gone."

Immediately she replied: "Don't worry, son. Today was the most important day of your life so far, but there are many, many days yet to come, and they will be even more important than this one."

I was stunned. As always, my mother was right. There would be—and still are—moments of happiness and success to come.

Some months later, the Latin Grammys were celebrated with a modest reception in LA. That night, we won Best New Artist, Best Rock Solo Vocal Album, and Best Rock Song.

The second album, *Un Día Normal*, was recorded in Los Angeles, again with Gustavo, Aníbal, and myself as producers. This time, everything was different—the energy, the enthusiasm . . . Now that the plane had taken off and the engines were running at full throttle, things were happening so quickly that I didn't have time to digest them.

During the recording sessions, I stayed at the Oakwood Apartments in LA, and Karen came with me for a few weeks. We were so in love, and at the same time my career was going better than ever.

One morning while checking my e-mail, I received a note from a great journalist friend of mine that said, "Juanes, congratulations on your daughter. She's such a cutie with her curly hair." I showed the e-mail to Karen and we both looked at each other as if to say, "How strange." I asked my friend why she wrote me this; later she replied, "Karen is pregnant with a baby girl." Just like that. And it turned out to be true! How did my friend know? I have no idea.

During the peak time of traveling and promoting *Un Día Normal*, our first child, Luna, was born. It's an indescribable moment. I knew instantly that my life had been split in two: before and after. And when I first held her in my arms in the hospital, I just couldn't believe it. I was the happiest man in the world.

Nevertheless, work continued at a frantic pace, and I was forced to divide my time between the joy of being a father for the first time and the stress of having to travel all the time. Karen was extremely brave and supportive in my times of absence during those first crucial months in our daughter's life.

Every time I returned home from the road, I had to make up for lost time. As she was growing up, Luna began to wonder why Dad was always coming and going. She repaid my absence with indifference, and it broke my heart, but all I could do was try to be the best father in the world with the small amount of time I was able to share with her.

"A Dios Le Pido," the first single from the album, came out, and it went straight to the top of the charts. I couldn't believe it. It seemed like a movie. There was an endless string of appearances, tours, concerts, a day in Argentina followed by breakfast in Madrid and lunch the next day in Germany. It was incredible: the fan base continued to grow; the label believed in us more and invested even more in the project.

With *Un Día Normal*, we toured the globe. I'd never been to so many places, and my energy was running at one hundred percent.

During the tour, I kept writing constantly. I always had my computer, my Pro Tools interface, a mini keyboard, and a few cables. Every hotel room became a mini traveling studio, and I recorded any and every idea that passed through my mind. Everything was so natural and pure, and my inspiration was at a max: the success of the album, my first experience as a father, the tour . . . Life was smiling upon me like never before, and that stirred a whole new wave of positive feelings within me.

The tour was two years of airplanes, long nights, and endless days of being away from my family. But when I went out onstage, the pain melted away. Those two hours out of the twenty-four in a day when I was feeling down and homesick were worth the sacrifice.

As soon as the tour had ended, and almost without stopping to catch my breath, I locked myself in the studio in my Coral Gables home to work on the demos that I'd brought back from the tour and build them into songs. I listed them by the names of the cities in which they were conceived—Bogotá, Amsterdam, Paris, Medellín, San Francisco, and so on—so I could remember what state of mind I was in at the time. I transcribed the guitar chords, the melodies, and the drums until the demo was finished. I asked Gustavo, Aníbal, and the rest of the team for permission to record in Miami so I could take advantage of that time to be close to my daughter and my wife, Karen, to whom I'd been happily married. Everyone agreed.

The follow-up album to *Un Día Normal* was called *Mi Sangre*. I recorded it in my garage, in the Hit Factory studios in Miami, and in an innumerable number of hotel rooms around the world. I didn't stop to rest for even a moment. I just couldn't. I was going through a period of such incredible effervescence that I couldn't let go. Plus, the creative juices were flowing freely. Songs like "Nada Valgo Sin Tu Amor," "Ámame," "La Camisa Negra," "Para Tu Amor"—which I wrote around the time of Luna's birth—were some of the tracks on the album, and I think they represent some of my best music.

We had barely finished recording *Mi Sangre* when we began promoting the album, and the travel involved was more uprooting and intense than ever. The idea was to ride the wave of the previous album in order to take full advantage of all the positive momentum we'd been building. I had to give an endless series of interviews all over the world, making for late nights of playing gigs, early morning flights, and more and more traveling. The only ones who suffered were my heart and my family at home. When I returned home on the weekends, it pained me to hear Karen's voice

on the verge of breaking, pretending that all was well. It was a very painful time, and it occasionally drove us to tears. I've since been able to recover some of the time I'd lost with my little Luna—thank God—but at the time it was not easy.

But all the work and sacrifices bore fruit. Soon enough, "La Camisa Negra" began to appear on the radio all over the world. I got fan mail from as far away as Morocco, Germany, Japan, and Australia, because people there were tuning in. I couldn't believe it. It had taken so long to reach this dream that once I made it into a reality, I had trouble believing it was really happening.

The international success and acclaim we received back then was enormous . . . so enormous that even today it's hard for me to take it all in.

With everything gaining so much strength, I was lucky that the record label, our management, my band, and I were all in total agreement on things. It made us unstoppable. There was no trip we wouldn't take, no concert we wouldn't attend, no interview we'd turn down. We did it all. I knew that if I didn't push hard even while everything was on the rise that I might just miss out on some of the biggest opportunities I'd ever have in my professional career.

But while my work was on the rise, my personal life was coming apart at the seams. Karen was raising our daughter as if she were a single mother, and deep in my heart it was tearing me to pieces. Despite all the happiness and benefits that came with it, my newfound success was nevertheless one of the greatest challenges of my life.

Paloma came into our lives as if to light our path even more. And the sweetness all made sense after seeing her birth.

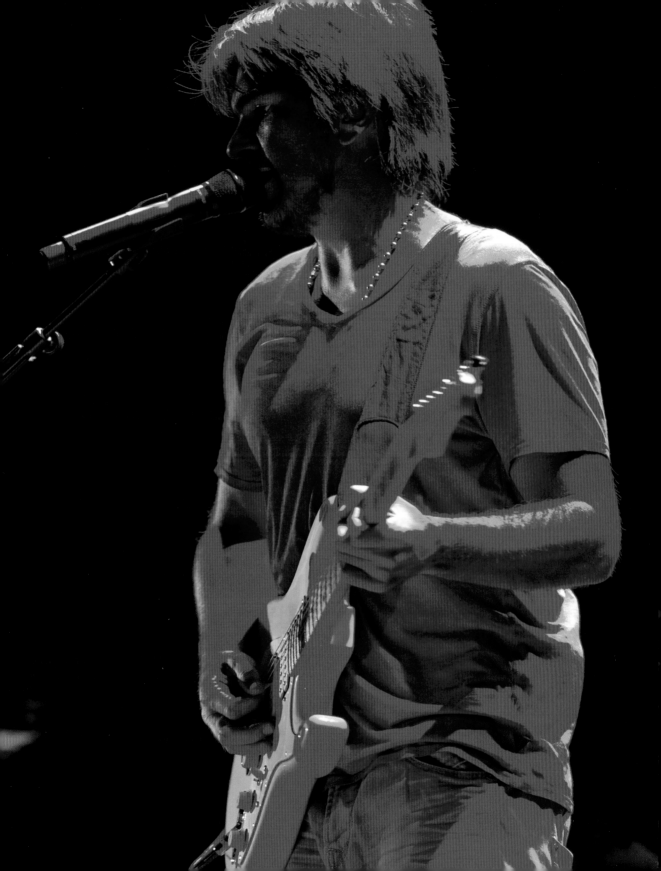

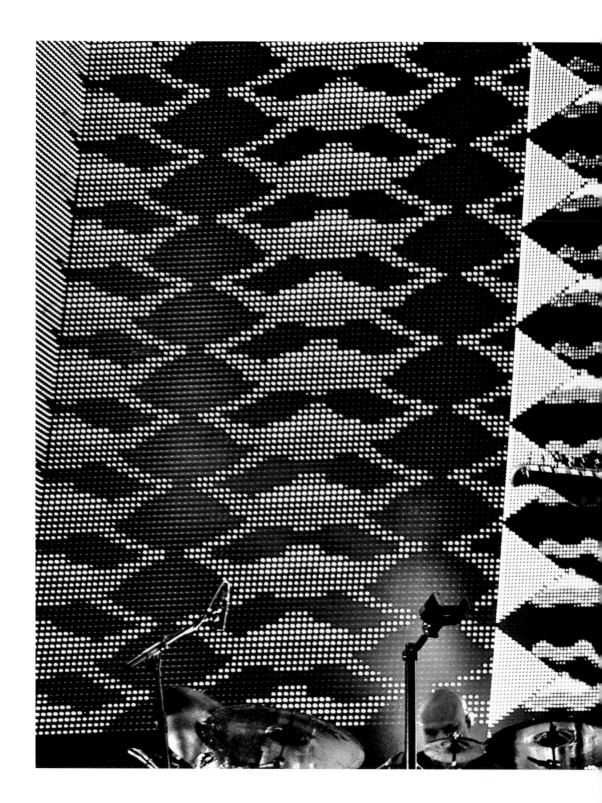

My beautiful Paloma was born on June 2, 2006. That day, I landed at the Miami airport at five in the morning after flying in from Venezuela. I went straight to the hospital, as Karen was already there with both our moms, being very well cared for, but still without me, and the baby was about to be born at any moment. Fortunately, I got there in time and was able to witness the birth with my wife.

Paloma was born that morning, and at three in afternoon I had to leave once again for Venezuela in order to finish the tour. After the happiness of being reunited with my family and the indescribable joy of welcoming our Paloma into the world, getting back on a plane was the absolute last thing I wanted to do. I felt like a convict being forced to do something against my will. It was a contradiction. The success I'd dreamed of all my life was destroying what I loved the most: time with my daughters and my wife.

It was easy enough to focus on work and convince myself that in some way my sacrifice would be worth all the pain, that it was an investment in the future of my family. But our separation was opening up tiny wounds that at first I couldn't—or didn't want to—see. I just kept on working, thinking that the more dedicated I was, the better it would be for everyone. We went on with the tour, and by the time we'd finished, we'd racked up another two years of concerts, trips, interviews, and good times . . . but also two more years' worth of distance.

Everything was going fine, and there was nothing to complain about, but inside I'd begun to feel the effects of mental and physical fatigue that comes with spending so much time on the road. What I didn't know was that it marked the beginning of a very dark time, and how much it would take to overcome it.

CROSSROADS

The *Mi Sangre* tour had ended, but my obsession with work had not. Three or four days removed from the wave of tours and travels, I once again shut myself up in the studio adjoining our house in Medellín, where we had recently moved. And though we were finally all together, my relationship with Karen was deteriorating due to distance and absence. The songs I was writing just weren't the same, and there were times in concert where I would find myself suffering from headaches and fatigue.

I worked all day in the studio, from eleven in the morning to eleven at night, again with the demos I'd made during the past two years on tour. I had to force myself to return to the house to eat or drink something, as if somehow the drive to succeed were pulling me in and wouldn't let me go. I worked constantly while my wife and daughters were getting used to their new life in Medellín. The girls were entering a new school, meeting new friends, and beginning a new routine, but despite all the challenges these changes involved, at least we were together. Or so we thought.

CROSSROADS | 167 | JUANES

A couple months later, everything began to collapse. My relationship with Karen was becoming more and more disconnected and I fell into such a deep state of confusion that it ended up costing me a separation that lasted nearly eight months. It was an impending tragedy, as if I were sitting in a plane watching as one of the engines burst into flames. Despite everything that was going on at the time, I still went to LA so I could show Gustavo the demo tapes to what would be my fourth album with him.

■

The success of "La Camisa Negra" was as wonderful as it was harmful. In the studio, forcing myself to prepare for my next album, I suddenly found myself thinking, *Now what do I do? If "La*

Camisa Negra" worked so well in Europe and the rest of the world, what should I do next? *More black shirts?* It was a question I couldn't get out of my head, as if there were a massive lion breathing down the back of my neck, about to devour me.

In LA, back in the studio with Gustavo, I was content but restless. I wasn't able to look into myself to figure out what exactly was going on, but something was definitely off. It didn't seem like anything serious; I just wasn't feeling quite right. It was just so hard to see the obvious: I had family problems that were eating me up inside.

After listening to the demos, Gustavo remained silent. I was watching him while we listened, but he didn't make eye contact with me. Until one point when he finally said, "Juanes, come—let's go for a walk in the park."

At that moment, I felt the universe collapsing around me. The nagging feelings I'd been having were more serious than I thought if they were affecting my creativity and music: the part of me that I always thought was unbreakable. My soul clenched.

Partway through the walk, Gustavo asked me, "Juanes, what sort of album do you want to make?"

And right then and there, I realized I didn't know the answer. I had no response. I tried to explain what was going on with success and how everything had shifted, and he understood. I'd lost my focus. I'd been trying to please others at my own expense.

We sat down on a bench high up on a mountain and talked for a long while about life and music before we returned to the studio. By then, I felt much more relaxed, and we had a deal: we would select the best demos to remix and rework, and focus on the lyrics, the melodies, and the structure.

That very same day, I flew back to Colombia to get back to work. Although my conversation with Gustavo had calmed me down and given me the confidence I needed to pick up the threads of what I'd been doing, I also felt a bit uneasy about what was happening to me. I had never felt this way before; music had always just flowed naturally from me, without requiring any force. But something had happened to me, and this wasn't the case anymore. I felt surrounded by silence and a tenacious sense of concern. I wasn't giving it my best—that much I knew—but I still felt that if I dedicated myself to the task at hand, I could still save something. I still had enough energy left to win.

I didn't leave the studio for two months. I worked like crazy, I didn't eat, I'd go to bed at five in the morning and wake up at eleven to get back to work. Karen and the girls decided to return to Miami, and I was left alone. Big mistake. That was where the problem began.

A couple of months later, I went back to Gustavo. Everything was a perfect match for the album, which ended up being called *La Vida Es un Ratico*. When it launched in 2007, four songs— "Me Enamora," "Gotas de Agua Dulce," "Tres," and the title track, "La Vida Es un Ratico"—were very well received by the press and by our fans.

It was my fourth album. I felt invincible, happy, and successful with the tours, the Grammys, and all the other accolades. And once again, the same promotional routine with the traveling, the interviews, and all that started up. But this time, I was facing the media frenzy with a gaping hole in my heart for not being on good terms with my wife and daughters. Before, when I was traveling, thinking of them was the engine that drove me forward, the light that brightened every moment of my day. But now, without them, nothing made sense. After several long months, I returned home, begged forgiveness for my absence, and we went back to being together, devoted to strengthening our relationship after all the harm done to ourselves and others.

We followed much the same path as we had on other tours. We played to exhaustion, we visited dozens of countries, we gave more interviews than ever, and the album was flying off the shelves, but I needed a break. Both my mind and my body were begging for some rest.

From a business standpoint, things worked like a charm. We announced a yearlong sabbatical, which would be tough, owing to my obsessive work ethic.

During that time of relative rest, my two daughters were growing up and my relationship with Karen got better and better. It took us some time to find our equilibrium, but with much patience and dedication we were gradually able to start communicating better and recover the sense of closeness we'd always had.

The sabbatical didn't last quite a year, be-

cause in 2009, I participated in the Peace Without Borders concert in Cuba. Even the planning was exciting. This concert would touch a different side of me, because it represented an intersection between art and social consciousness. That sense of responsibility to end the injustices we see in our lives really grew within me and ended up materializing in the creation of the Mi Sangre Foundation.

In between trips and visits home, I was still trying to write new songs, but something felt wrong. My creativity was spent and repetitive. Nevertheless, I pressed on without quite being able to see the alarms going off. I was busy with the concert in Cuba, with composing my new album, and with my most sacred and important creation: the birth of my first son, Dante.

While Dante was still in the womb, I traveled to Havana, Madrid, and Bogotá, and on the rare occasions when I found myself in the studio, I was still striving to find what might be the songs for my upcoming album. But despite the fact that my personal life was, as it were, restored, new, and complete again, I didn't feel satisfied with what I'd achieved.

Dante was born on September 12, 2009, just eight days before I would have to fly to Cuba for

the concert. Dante's birth and the concert in Cuba became a watershed event that defined my life. It was as if an unexpected force I never knew I had crashed over me in a powerful, definitive wave. Those two events, only eight days apart, generated a compelling change inside me.

The concert in Cuba showed me the two sides of every coin—love and hate, right and wrong, lies and truth—and I witnessed the frustration and ultimately the joy of seeing over a million Cubans singing and smiling. Cuba taught me how to recognize true friends.

With Dante, I too felt reborn, with a new spiritual and karmic connection with my dad, as if the father-son cycle closes itself in order to create something impenetrable.

In December of 2009, I went to London to meet with Steve Lipson, the producer of my new project, which would be called *P.A.R.C.E.* Everything in my life had changed: internally I was enduring an inexplicable sense of malaise, and the pressure from the record label and from the management team was incessant. "You have to work, you have to produce something" was all I ever heard.

As much as things weren't right inside of me, my daughters and my family gave me strength. Everything would be all right. If four albums had turned out okay, why not this one? I worked on the demos and spent time with my family. Damage had been done to my relationship with my wife, but thanks to God and time, the wound was beginning to heal.

Among the things that were not working well for me—that, like me, were out of focus—was the 2010 World Cup in South Africa. I didn't much enjoy the experience. I wasn't prepared to be there; the song wasn't right, nor was the moment—mistakes that only now, in hindsight, I understand and accept. The next day, I was on a plane flying to London via Paris, I hadn't seen a single match, and I had to swallow the bitter pill of not having the right song at the right time—the result of lacking the guts to do something and my fight against arrogance that often rears its head in the artistic world and in life itself.

London was a painful, solitary, and dry process, like walking for hours across the desert without a drop to drink. In my soul, in my heart, in my desire but inability to do things differently, every-thing was interiorized; nothing was out in the open. I was a pris-oner of my own invention, chained to fear and tired of it all, on the verge of exploding. Eight years of wonderful work, success, and happiness came at a very steep personal and creative price. Basi-cally, I hated myself. I was overexposed, and almost burnt to a crisp.

The recording process with Mr. Lipson was pleasant, if solitary. He didn't speak Spanish, so I tried to explain the lyrics, but they never sounded as strong in English as they did in the original. We worked in the studio from Monday to Friday, and on the weekends I would walk around the city feeling so lost and down that I didn't even bother calling friends to make plans. It was my solitude and myself, asking questions, looking to the sky and saying, *God, what's wrong with me?* From time to time, I'd share my concerns with Karen.

In the studio, either the songs worked or they didn't. That's how it is, yes, but I'd tried each song a thousand different times. I was driving myself crazy, and drinking a bottle of wine a day to supposedly relax me. Nah, it was just a lie—things were so bad that anything and everything made my situation even worse. Only Karen and I knew this.

I finished recording the album and it was released in December of that same year, six months after the World Cup. The songs were no good at all, I was worse than ever, and I couldn't bear to look at myself in the mirror, let alone see myself on TV or in a magazine. I was overworked, and to make matters worse I had a new album in stores that didn't represent me and instead revealed the clear signs of wear and tear. At this point, I felt completely alone, lacking the support of my team.

■

This was a painful birthing process, one filled with personal growth. Mentally, I had gone to the edge of the cliff and felt obliged to jump. That feeling was expanding inside of me, and only my wife and family knew about it. I was on the verge of exploding. The tour began amid uncertainty and bad vibes among the team.

In Seattle, our first show, during my normal walk from the dressing room to the stage, I felt the heavy weight of the atmosphere and nostalgia for the old days. I wasn't asking for much. The show was all right—not much of anything, really, other than evidence of what was to come: a difficult tour, lousy album sales, internal conflicts among the team . . . and me, exhausted.

We went out onstage to start the show, and there I was, looking out over all the attendees. I looked behind me and saw myself surrounded by giant screens projecting images of the band and crowd, and everything seemed to come to life despite all the difficulties. But I still felt the weight of the chains, and I said to myself, "I don't know how much longer I can bear this."

The tour went on to San Francisco, Los Angeles, and other cities across the United States.

In San Francisco, I was walking with my wife and kids through the security checkpoint toward our gate when out of nowhere came a woman in her fifties who apparently recognized me and said to me in Spanish: "I have to tell you something. Please don't be frightened. I had a dream about you, and now that I've got you here in front of me, I have to tell you about it." I felt chills and replied, "You had a

dream about me? Are you serious? I hope it wasn't a nightmare at least!" And I smiled.

The woman explained that the same thing had happened with another person several months back, and later it came true. She told me that I'd have a fight with someone close to me, that I would go through a time of great trials and tribulations, but that I would emerge and move on. "Jesus, are you serious? You believe this stuff?" I replied. The woman simply replied that sometimes these things happen, and she just had to say something about it.

We landed in LA around noon, and we wanted to get something to eat before going to the Staples Center for the sound check. I felt sick and exhausted in my soul. Fortunately for me, my wife and three children were with me.

We went to a restaurant downtown and Rubi, who worked with us, said to my wife: "Hey, look at that girl up on the balcony there. There's something strange about her." Things continued normally—we sat down at a table, ordered our food, chatted.

Minutes later, a very pleasant server came up to us and said, "Juanes, when you're ready to leave, please use the door in the back of the restaurant." I asked him why, but he just motioned his hand from left to right across his neck as if to say, "Don't ask me."

The twentysomething girl whom Rubi had mentioned had jumped to her death right there in the restaurant parking lot, just a few feet away from our car. Shocked and shaken, we got in the car as quickly as possible, with Karen trying to distract Paloma while Rubi

and I tried to keep Dante and Luna from looking. As the car pulled away, I could see the girl's body, covered in a white sheet, receding in the rearview mirror.

A couple of police cars and a few curious passersby . . . All afternoon I was asking myself, *What made that girl jump off that balcony? Why end it like that? How desperate do you have to be . . . ?*

On the drive to the concert, everything was stunned silence. I'm very superstitious; I don't walk under ladders, and if I see a black cat crossing the road, I turn around. So this suicide had really shaken me. In a matter of minutes, right in front of my family, a girl had jumped to her death. It was as if everything had been set up for us to witness it.

We entered the concert venue and—unbeknownst to me—none of the motors that move the giant screen panels around were working. Nobody had said a word, so as not to worry me. Bad decision. We did our sound check, and I could sense that there was something wrong with the screens, but I hadn't been notified of any problems. Ten minutes before the show, in my dressing room, I was told about the problem, and the ground fell out from under me. My first thought was of the girl who'd jumped. Is there anything more ominous to see on the day of your concert? Of course something was going to go wrong.

I argued with a few of the roadies, but there was nothing they could do. It was five minutes to showtime. I turned to my friends and family and said, "I can't believe that on one of the most important shows of the whole tour, this happened. This just can't be happening." I felt overwhelmed, confused, consumed by the anger and frustration about not being able to do anything. I walked up to the stage, accompanied by my bandmates, who had become like members of my family.

There, backstage, Waldo Madera, our bassist, whom I deeply respect for his talent, grabbed my arm and said without a hint of reservation: "Bro, don't forget that you're a musician. Forget about the big screens and all that. Our show is about musicians and music. Stay calm and the crowd won't even know the difference."

Wise words, and well timed, too. The fans were ready to rock, and so we ran out onstage. Despite a difficult situation, the place was packed that night, and the concert got some of the best reviews I've ever had in that city. It was a success.

That night, in the second row at the Staples Center, an elderly man, perhaps in his seventies, gave me the strength to succeed. It was one of those moments in which an isolated and otherwise inconsequential act comes alive and provides us with a vital and necessary lesson. I was singing and playing my guitar, running from one side of the stage to the other with all the energy I could muster, and all of a sudden I saw this old guy there, dancing and singing like there was no tomorrow. He was an inspiration to me.

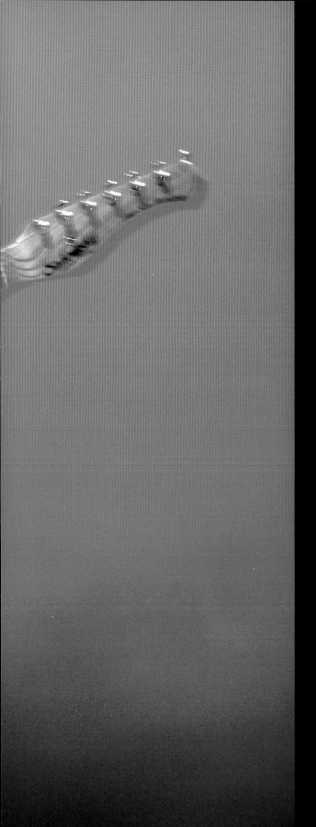

I thought about all the strange signs from throughout the day: the woman at the security checkpoint, the girl who took her own life at the restaurant, the equipment that didn't work, the discussion in the dressing room with the crew and staff, and finally the seventy-something man who ultimately—along with the rest of the wonderful crowd that night—took away all those bad vibes.

■

The energy that gentleman displayed in the audience that night got me thinking about all the young people I've come to know through the Mi Sangre Foundation, which we established in 2006. It's amazing how something as ordinary as someone dancing at a show can send us signals that are so vital that they end up mobilizing our lives and the lives of others.

Many years before, when *Fíjate Bien* first came out, with its message about the problems of antipersonnel mines in Colombia, I received requests from both state and private organizations to link my name to campaigns raising awareness about the issue. I then had the opportunity to learn about that reality up close and personal and get to know the true pains suffered by the victims of these mines. I felt I had to do something, so in 2006 I made the decision to create the Mi Sangre Foundation to do more specific and concrete work to address the problem.

That's how we started focusing on developing programs to aid mine victims both physically and emotionally. I felt the need to help heal the wounds in their souls that—while invisible—run deep and contribute to the vicious cycle of violence. We undertook the challenge of bringing to light a problem that very few people in the country were aware of.

We organized a charity concert in Los Angeles called Colombia Without Mines, and in 2009 we were able to finally give a voice to the victims through the Ottawa Convention, also known as the Anti-Personnel Mine Ban Convention.

It's been a path of much learning, of much connecting with the pain of fellow Colombians, and of much conviction in the power we have as human beings to transform our reality. As such, we've since redefined the focus of our foundation to include all young people who have been affected by any form of violence, or who are at risk. Besides providing physical and psychological care, we've developed an educational program to teach peace through art in order to transcend the image of victimization and help people become peacemakers.

Like me, many young people today find their inspiration in music or other forms of artistic expression. So it's worth it to invest in education and the arts, because it's our way of narrating ourselves, of thinking about ourselves, of opposing violence, and above all it's our way of never forgetting. With its inherent sensitivity, art can mobilize much more so than reason. It creates consciousness and connects worlds, because, in essence, it's universal, it's diverse.

Since the Mi Sangre Foundation began, I've met many young people who are now friends and colleagues. Through art, they are connecting themselves responsibly to their communities, their histories, and the construction of their own futures. Little by little, I've come to see just how many people who, despite their anger and pain, have been able to change hatred into love and are intent on building a greater peace.

The young people involved in our foundation have inspired me with their courage. In the face of all the adversity and the violence in their neighborhoods, they still get up each and every morning and choose a microphone or a guitar instead of a weapon. They are artists who transcend the violent reality of their lives and—not content with seeing death and inequality in their cities—are betting on a better life.

The value placed on change by all those who work with the foundation is what had been missing from my professional life.

I was so keyed in to long debates with the label and with promoters . . . *Why this? Why that? What if we do this?* Ultimately, it was awful. We were reaching the end of our U.S. tour; only Miami and Orlando were left, and they would end up getting canceled.

The final show would be in Washington, D.C., a concert I particularly enjoyed. I don't know if it was the nostalgia or the energy that day . . . Onstage, it looked like I had the energy of a raging bull, but my heart was sick and sad. That night, I had sent a text that went something like this: *I don't know whether this will be the last night I ever sing onstage again.* But I was very wrong. The show was a smashing success and the reviews, again, were great. I felt like I was receiving signs and messages from everywhere.

I returned home after a month and a half on the road. I spent two or three days searching for rest I simply could not find. My only thought was how I could end my remaining commitments; we had barely begun what would be yet another long, arduous tour.

I talked with my wife, my brother, and my mom. They could sense that something wasn't right, but they didn't pry into it. I felt soulless, as if my faith were just lying there on the floor while I walked around the house like an emotionless zombie. My children and my wife were my only anchor.

One day, after our last show in D.C., I woke up listless, took a shower, and remembered that my wife had fixed the mirror. I stepped out of the shower and peered into it. I couldn't recognize myself. I couldn't take this. I needed to stop for a moment, reconsider some things, get myself together, and above all listen to that little voice inside me which I'd all but turned off. My relationship with God had grown strained; I wanted to find fault with anything and everything, and my sense of faith was at an all-time low.

I stared at myself in the mirror and exploded. *Enough! I've gotta put a stop to it!*

I called my manager and we had a six-hour meeting in which I explained my personal and emotional state. I said I wouldn't be doing any work in the immediate future. I needed it to stop.

We met at a small restaurant in my neighborhood in Miami, and just as I was pulling in, I looked up and saw a big red traffic sign that read STOP. I grinned and thought to myself, *Wow—that's a sign if ever there was one!*

The next day, I called my bandmates and e-mailed the other members of the team. I spoke with the president of the record label and asked him to let everyone who worked with me know that we were going to take a break for a while. Not for long, but for an indefinite amount of time. It could be a few months, but ultimately it would be whatever my body and soul needed, not what some external figure decided.

At this point in the road, I had to let go of all the chains and weights that had been holding me down and making life next to impossible. I had been a puppet whose strings were being pulled by someone else. My sadness ran deep: for the first time in my life, I felt defeated, and I couldn't see the future clearly at all.

It was around that time that I read a quote from Pope John Paul II: "In order to have everything, you must renounce everything." That's pretty much what I felt I needed to do. When I asked my mother for her opinion, she didn't hesitate: "Son, you've been putting off this break for much too long. Stay home and spend more time with your kids. Everything will be okay."

I spoke with my brother José, who's in charge of my finances, and I asked him the same thing. "Juan," he said, "take it easy—we've got it all under control. It's not a problem at all. Take some time to rest and recuperate."

The response from Jesús López, president of the record company, was almost the same: "Juan, we need you whole. Take your time and organize your thoughts. The company will always be here to support you." And that was it. My friends in the band were worried about work, but they understood. And the label was behind me as well.

The only one who didn't agree was my manager at the time. We all have our own reasons, our own projects, our own paths to travel— as we all should. But when those paths lead in different directions, then it's time to part ways. It happens to everyone at one time or another. These are the crossroads that point us to new horizons.

I still remember the feeling of lightness I felt when I walked out of that meeting with my now ex-manager. As I rode my bike home, I said to myself, I have finally listened to my heart . . . Now I'm the one in charge of my life and my time.

Some people told me I was crazy, that in a matter of minutes I'd just thrown my entire career out the window. But inside I felt strong and free. The best is always yet to come.

NEW DAY

After hitting rock bottom, in 2011 I embarked on a fascinating search for my faith and my own self. I had lost my center, and now I had to rescue myself . . . What better way to do it than being around my family and friends? So that's exactly what I did.

I began a regimen of absolute detox: I shut down my e-mail account, I changed my phone number, and I kept out of the public eye. The only things I left active were my Twitter account and my Facebook page, so I could keep in touch with my fans. I could imagine all the speculation about the changes I'd made, and I didn't want any rumors going around.

Even though I asked a person I trusted to be discreet, the calm lasted only a few days. Then the attacks from news outlets started coming—attacks that hurt both me and my family.

One day, I was checking my Twitter account and found a series of statements from my former manager. I couldn't believe what I was reading. It filled me with such sadness and frustration, although I could understand where his pain was coming from. Without giving it too much thought, I replied publicly to his comments, explaining why I needed a bit of a break.

The media reaction was immediate. I kept quiet and hung in there while watching all sorts of false allegations come to the surface: they said that I had left the music scene completely, that I'd become a Christian, that I'd gone bankrupt, that I was suffering from a mental disease . . . It would be hard to say which story was the most ludicrous!

Even though the media's response was so absurd, I had to constantly remind myself that I was at home, completely confident about the decision I'd made, and at peace while the outside world was a tornado of chaos and speculation. I'd turn on the TV and see allegedly good friends offering comments without having any idea of what was really going on. It was completely crazy. I was hurt, but I ultimately understood that that's how the world works, and so it's best to focus on changing your own inside world and not anyone else's.

During this time, I worked in the studio and had surgery on my right knee, which had been taking a lot of wear and tear over the years. I've enjoyed exercising ever since I was fifteen years old, because I was overweight when I was younger. No matter where in the world I found myself, every day of my life I'd hit the streets for a forty-five-minute run. But eventually, the day came when my knee was clamoring for a little care of its own.

It was in May that the news came of lawyers wanting to meet to determine whether my decisions represented a breach of contract. The shows in Orlando and Miami had been canceled, but the promoter of those events had understood my situation and there had been no fallout. All that was left was the Spain tour in July and August, but since that was still months away, I decided I could wait things out and see what happened.

■

The next few months were time for meditation and confrontation. I read all sorts of books, watched movies and documentaries, worked in the studio, limped around the house with my crutches (and even limped around the airport occasionally when I had to travel somewhere). I never stopped keeping busy, but the difference this time was that every moment now was about *me*.

I slowly regained control of my time and my life, got things back on my terms, and now I wasn't having to fulfill the expectations of someone else telling me, "You are a product." Comments like those had hurt me deeply, but in a sense they had been true: that's exactly what I was, a toy that would go this way and that without knowing why, simply following the incessant rhythms of a rotten, mechanized system.

But while some people called me a coward for leaving everything, others understood my reasoning and knew what was right. I felt brave; I never imagined I'd be capable of such a thing as firing my manager, saying good-bye to my musician friends, asking my production company for a break, leaving the commodity behind, let alone the constant stream of money.

It wasn't easy, but it was a crucial point in my existence, a rebirth that brought with it both maturity and suffering. I got all the cheap and ridiculous thoughts out of my mind. I started to remember who I really was, the essence of my childhood, the values I was raised with, and, more important, my faith in God, which had grown worn and distant.

I spent those months meditating, walking, reading the Bible and parts of the Koran as well as poetry and novels, playing the guitar, and working in the studio a little each day. I couldn't exercise too much because of my knee surgery, but I was finding the peace I'd been searching for.

At what moment had I allowed this to happen? How had things gotten to this point? There was only one answer: ambition and a lack of courage. You are the only one who can answer the questions that life asks of you. Not even your most trusted friends can do this for you. Your heart is the only thing that knows the truth.

I grew closer to God, but this time there was more certainty in my mind and in my soul about who I really was. I connected with Jesus and read books in search of answers about life and the universe. I had a bad relationship with the church but great respect for the religion, and I finally understood I had the free will and ability to distinguish between the two and say, *Okay, this is what I believe and this is what I'm going to do.*

I spoke with many people. They all had different thoughts and opinions and would offer me different sorts of advice, but deep inside I was confident I'd made a decision that would allow me to start anew, to follow my path to happiness. Not the happiness of others. My own. That was my only goal: to get rid of every obstacle between me and my own happiness.

Even amid all this introspection, there was never a time when I wasn't working on my songs. Music has always been a part of my everyday life, and eliminating it would have driven me insane. But I have to admit that there were nights filled with uncertainty and questions about the future of my career, my music, and my creativity. With all the talk flying around, people would ask me, "Is it true you're retiring?" People are so prone to believing the rumors!

It seemed others were intent on making me look like I was mentally unstable, a depressed madman who had canceled sixty concerts. Of course, that was completely off base. I wasn't sick in the head; I was healing and finding my own path, free from fear.

Time passed and my personal life improved. I was certain, deep in my soul, that I had done the right thing. Maybe it cost me some career opportunities, but at the time the most important thing for me to do was to stop—for the sake of both myself and my sense of creativity.

I thought a lot about the type of career that I wanted and the sort of artist I wanted to be. In order to confront my fears head-on, I cleared my mind of all preconceptions, which allowed me to find the answers I was looking for. I wanted to return to the scene knowing fully well that I would never retire permanently from music and that I had just been looking for a little break. Nobody else could understand those moments; nobody else was inside me when I was enduring them.

Even though we work, have obligations, and have goals to achieve in life, we cannot forget that we are people with feelings, and that even when we have a certain degree of power over others, there are no circumstances when it's okay to mistreat or abuse someone. I felt that that's what had been

done to me, and the crisis I had to go through was my response to the corrupt system in which we live.

It's not all bad when you're going through tough times. You can learn a lot from life and from other people. You come to realize the reasons why certain people surround you. It's really amazing how folks can show their true colors in times of difficulty. It's definitely a good idea to do a little housecleaning from time to time.

◼

July was approaching, and it was time for the Spain tour to begin. For me it was pure bliss, absolute joy, a reunion with the truth, the fans, and the music. I was once again able to enjoy my own music, my passion. I fell in love with my guitar again. All the nonsense that had come out through the press, my former colleagues, and the critics had affected me deeply. And I saw I'd been trying to make music in line with certain trends and marketing schemes; this also had wounded me deeply. Ultimately, I had been betraying myself.

My biggest hits, like "Yerbatero," "La Camisa Negra," and "A Dios Le Pido," had come from my soul. They were completely natural, and that's why they'd gone where they did. Later, I made the mistake of trying to fit myself into artificial patterns. For example, *P.A.R.C.E.* ended up being more

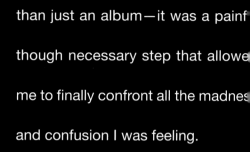

than just an album—it was a painf

though necessary step that allowe

me to finally confront all the madnes

and confusion I was feeling.

The Spain tour lasted a month, an

when it was over, I felt as though I ha

gained control of my life again. And be

cause life works this way sometimes,

also happened to get an invitation fror

MTV to do an unplugged album high

ghting my career, and—why not?—

maybe we'd toss in a few unreleased

racks to boot? A bright light had ap-

peared in the midst of all that darkness,

and even though it was unexpected, it

looked like it could be part of a great

destiny. I talked with José Tillán, presi-

dent of MTV Tr3s and a great friend

who has supported my career from day

one, and we visualized the project.

I was dreaming about music again.

A year and a half earlier, at an event for Cadena Ser in Tenerife, I'd found myself backstage with Miguel Bosé, Ricky Martin, and Juan Luis Guerra. My good friend Amarilys Germán, Juan Luis's manager, was there too, and she'd said something that really struck me: "Why don't you ask Juan Luis to see if he'd produce an album for you? You guys should work together."

My eyes opened wide and I answered without a shadow of a doubt: "Ama, are you serious? I'm gonna go ask him right now!"

So I did. Quietly and nervously, I went over to Juan Luis as he was talking with Miguel and Ricky, and I said, "Maestro, would you like to produce an album for me?"

"It would be an honor," he replied.

Nearly two years had passed between the time when I'd spoken with Juan Luis and Amarilys

and when MTV asked me about doing an unplugged album. But now the first thing that came to mind was to call Amarilys and ask her about working with Juan on the project.

Ama happened to be in Miami on business, so we met up at the Biltmore Hotel in Coral Gables. From there—she with a cup of coffee, and me with a glass of champagne to calm my nerves—we called Juan Luis, who was in the Dominican Republic working on another project.

Ama told him about MTV, then handed me the phone. I told him a little more about the idea. His reply was slow and calm: "Let's do it, Juanes."

■

In September, we made some public appearances, including the Pan-American Games in Mexico, where I sang "Odio Por Amor." In August, we'd been to Geneva, the Nansen Awards, and a few other things.

On that trip to Geneva, something happened that has had a permanent impact on my life. It occurred one night at the hotel, and the timing couldn't have been better. I was jet-lagged and

couldn't sleep after the event, so I called the room where a few of my bandmates were staying up on the tenth floor with a balcony overlooking Lake Geneva. There were four or five of us talking about the show, about how good it had been, and about the energy we were feeling with the new team. It was one of those priceless

moments that, considering the months of difficulty, allowed us to feel a connection again. We were talking about the importance of love and life and good vibes, about how vital it is to feel good about yourself so you can project that feeling to others.

I was looking out over the lake and the sky when suddenly I saw five airplanes that looked as if they were about to land at the Geneva airport—at least that's what I thought at first. But they were so big and low and lit up the lonely silent night. They weren't moving. "Hey, guys," I said, "check that out—doesn't that look kind of weird?" They seemed like airplanes, and yet they weren't moving forward or backward.

One of the bandmates said, "What are they, helicopters?"

"Hot-air balloons?" suggested another.

In a matter of moments, we went from doubt and speculation to absolute certainty. What we were witnessing wasn't normal. Almost in unison, we all said, "Bro, they're definitely UFOs!" We were all yelling with excitement at having witnessed such a spectacular event in the skies over Geneva.

We watched as they moved laterally in absolute silence, as if they were being controlled by a computer or a GPS system. It was unbelievable!

The lights would move and then stop for minutes at a time before starting to move again. All told, it lasted about fifteen or twenty minutes. I noticed that they seemed to move in geometric patterns, just as I'd seen other UFOs make in videos online. Two of them took off at an incredible speed, leaving three larger lights hanging there in the shape of a perfect triangle. A minute or two later, they disappeared into the night as well.

I've always believed in extraterrestrial life. In fact, I stay up at night watching documentaries and reading books about it. So you can imagine what that moment meant to me.

We shouted with excitement. I was mesmerized and thrilled—I'd just witnessed something I'd believed in for so many years. I called my wife, who was also excited, though in a different way. I think she was so petrified that she almost had a heart attack!

That night, I wondered whether we were the only ones to have seen it. Had there been any other witnesses? Would it be on the news tomorrow? But the next morning, there wasn't the slightest tidbit about it in the local papers, on TV, or even online. Zero. Not a word.

My head started spinning with all sorts of questions about my education, my religion, the church, the government, the media . . . My mind was ablaze, as if my whole structure was rife with doubt and on the verge of collapse. What is the true source of our creation? What or who were those lights in the sky? Why have so many people experienced similar things?

Before, I had been convinced that we weren't alone in the universe, but I didn't have a clear understanding of it. But after that night, everything seemed to fall into place: my empirical theories about life and creation, about man's behavior on earth, about mental disease, about the decline of our current societies . . . everything.

Calmly, on my balcony back at home, I stared at the moon and the stars through a telescope I'd gotten for Christmas, and I thought about how stupid I'd been. It was obvious that we were not alone. It is only the pride and ego of humankind that prevents us from accepting the fact that we are a part of something greater than ourselves. We are but a tiny part of a vast universe that we know so little about, and yet we live our lives narrowly in a world where the only thing that matters is how much you have, because that makes you who you are.

I came back from Geneva shaken to the core, and more determined than ever to continue recovering what I'd lost and, little by little, regain control of my life and career.

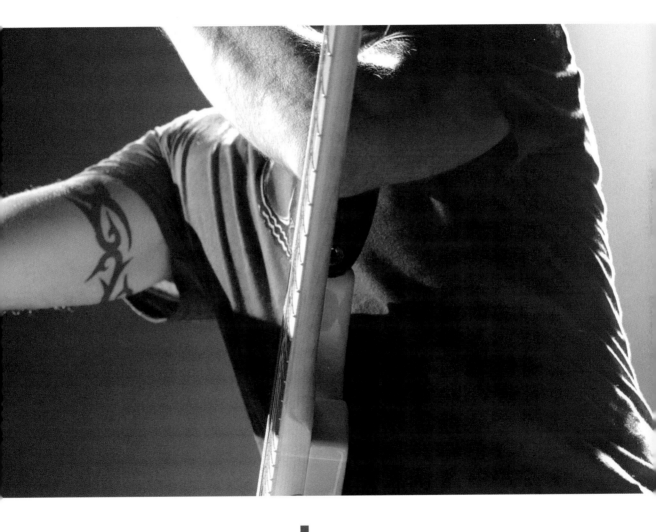

By the end of October, plans with MTV were moving along nicely and it seemed that my dream of doing an unplugged album would become a reality.

JUANES MTV UNPLUGGED

The fact that the great maestro Juan Luis Guerra had agreed to work with me as producer was nothing less than magical—a true blessing that filled me with inspiration and proved that I had done the right thing by moving forward with my career and my music.

By then, I was already feeling more calm and relaxed, so I decided to compose the songs along the inspirational idea of what it means to truly unplug yourself. I spoke a bit with the band members in order to shore up the staff; I've always counted on the support of some good friends who didn't leave me hanging during that difficult period of time. With them by my side, the road ahead was clear.

By the time November and December rolled around, I had my new team in place, my new manager, my new life, my new dreams . . . But, most important, I had control. Control over my own life.

We worked nonstop on all fronts to make sure that this MTV idea would become a reality. Every so often I'd meet up with Juan Luis in the Dominican Republic to listen to his new ideas and talk about the album's concept, how we were going to achieve it, and which musicians and guests to invite.

We had a few rehearsals in Miami, where Juan Luis recorded almost every song. Those were long, hard rehearsals involving a lot of precision but also a lot of freedom. Juan would sit on a sofa and just listen. He let us work while he observed. Things were getting more advanced, more

polished, and we as a band were touching up every last detail. We'd change chords or structures, but mostly we listened closely to Juan Luis's advice.

We learned a lot of things during those months. Later we were joined by Joaquín Sabina and Paula Fernández to create two of the most beautiful duets of my career: "Hoy Me Voy" with Paula and "Azul Sabina" with the master Joaquín.

I also delighted in the opportunity to compose a couple of songs with the one and only Juan Luis Guerra. It was something truly beautiful, like playing fast and easily. I was more than a little nervous, while Juan Luis was totally calm and confident.

On one of those afternoons in Juan Luis's home studio in the Dominican Republic, I witnessed how he worked, his love for his guitars, and how seriously he took his life in music. For me, this was an absolute inspiration. I watched him and thought, *My God, there's so much left that I still want to do! I want to have a career as long, serious, and lasting as this great man of music.* I sometimes referred to him affectionately as the fifth Beatle.

A few days after I returned home from the Dominican Republic, I started to reorganize my office. I took my guitars cleaned them one by one. I untangled the cables and reconnected the microphones that I'd stored away. It was a rebirth, a reawakening, a new way to see my life and my career, a new way to interpret music.

We worked constantly and rehearsed tire-lessly through the end of the year. I traveled to Colombia for a few days with my family to rest up and reflect.

On January 2, 2012, I flew from Cartagena to the Dominican Republic for one of the most important meetings of that time of my life: a session with Juan Luis to coordinate all the last-minute details for the MTV special and to brainstorm a few final ideas. During that trip, I put the finishing touches on "Azul Sabina" and "Todo en Mi Vida Eres Tú." After that, we had the last few rehearsals in Miami. We were only a month away from showtime.

We practiced every day from around noon to all hours of the night. It was hard work, but I was happy. I woke up with an ear-to-ear smile on my face just as I did when I was a kid

"No es solo un deseo, es el sueño de todo un p
¡Vamos Colombia!"

Mariana Pajón y Jose Lu
BMX

starting out with my band in Medellín. I knew that soon I'd be singing and strumming alongside the best musicians in the business, under the direction of the greatest of them all, Juan Luis Guerra. I was living a dream that continues to this day.

After an intense month of practice and tune-ups, we went to the New World Symphony in Miami to record the *MTV Unplugged* show. We had a general rehearsal on February 1, and then made the final recording the following day. There was tension and excitement, but everything was under control. Everyone knew exactly what to do, and since we had rehearsed under strict supervision, we would be calm and composed when it came time to record.

Minutes before we were to take the stage, Juan Luis asked everyone involved in the project—musicians, technicians, guests—to get together for a prayer. It was a beautiful moment that I'll never forget. We all closed our eyes and listened attentively to Juan Luis's words. When he finished, we applauded him and headed out onstage.

In the moments before a concert, I've often thought about what I was doing there when instead I could have a simple life planting yuca or potatoes in some farm in the mountains without the pressures and responsibilities that come with having such a public life and profession. But it's the adrenaline and the nerves that connect you so directly to music and people.

I walked through a small door facing the stage, and immediately I smiled with gratitude. I looked all across the people in attendance and thanked them for being there. Those few seconds just before beginning the first song always seem infinite. I picked up my guitar, situated it comfortably, and sat down on the stool. We started to play.

The session was magnificent, and the project itself was a new composition, as if on that night I had been reborn as a musician. It was a wonderful celebration full of hugs and old friends, including journalists, musicians, and people from the music industry. I think I was the last one to leave that night, because I didn't want it to end.

But it did.

A few close friends came back to the hotel with us—friends who had been with us throughout all of this. Among them was my respected colleague and dear friend Fonseca, along with Rebeca, Chris, Olguita . . . ultimately, the people I love so much.

■

Half an hour later, someone said, "Hey, Juanes, we gotta start the phone in-terviews." I wanted to roll over and die. I was so exhausted, having already had a full day of in-person interviews.

I took the phone. My voice was half hoarse from the session and half hoarse from the after-party the night before. This particular interview went well, all the questions were respectful and intelligent, and just when I thought it was over the journalist said, "Juanes, this next question comes from the stars. There's a listener who wants to know about your experience with UFOs."

Although I had my doubts about this alleged listener—very few people knew about my interest in the subject, since I didn't want any misunderstandings to become news—I wasn't quite quick enough to handle this twist in the interview. Seeing no malicious intent, I answered as simply as I could, politely finished the story, and moved on from there.

At the end of the day, tired as a dog, I met up with the people from the record label to take stock of things and to thank the people who had worked with me for so many years, from the president of the company to all the regional executives.

It was at that meeting that I realized I'd been fooled. The six o'clock news was doing a story about *MTV Unplugged*, but it wasn't exactly about the tremendous show we'd put on. It was about my experience with UFOs. Most of the media outlets also ran the story—some in jest, others respectfully—and in the end they all mentioned the album. I was upset at first, but then I realized the intent of this little game: overshadowing the real news, which was recording an unplugged album for MTV.

I went home a bit disgruntled, but with a sense of happiness that nothing could take away from me . . . not even the headlines about UFOs. I was content and grateful to God for allowing me to accomplish such a thing with so many important and talented people.

My whole way of looking at life had changed after that trip to Geneva. Now, when I look up at the sky, it's not in the hopes of seeing more UFOs; it's to see my faith, strong and renewed. And in the end, I know the truth of what I saw there.

■

The months following the *MTV Unplugged* recording were all about planning, meetings, appointments, photo ops . . . not much action, but a lot of excitement. I felt happy and recharged and I didn't want to stop working. I kept writing new songs and enjoying my family life as never before, because I knew that sooner or later I was going to catch one of those waves that keep me away from home for days at a time.

Promotion time came, and we started our endless string of trips and interviews. We spent three months visiting Spain, Argentina, the United States, Brazil, Colombia, Mexico, and Venezuela, reconnecting with our fans by playing for them in small, intimate events.

I really enjoyed those trips, as they helped me continue living my dream of being a musician and, even more, they allowed me to feel the love of my people—fans and the media included—despite the speculations and rumors from a few bad apples who just wanted to make me look sick, crazy, and depressed.

God is great, and all this time I've spent finding myself has allowed me to strengthen my inner self, to fight my fears and take them down. There may be other artists in this world who don't have to go through phases like this in their lives, but for me it was a matter of life or death. It was a necessary point in my learning process, a required rearrangement of my life and career. During that time, I focused on getting to know myself better on the inside, because I knew that I've been able to mature and grow and change into the person I am now: balanced, satisfied, and completely happy.

REFLECTION

Right now I'm sitting in my living room in Medellín, putting the final touches to this story that I thought I'd never tell. I've searched and reached into the deepest parts of my memory in the hopes of illustrating my path and sharing my history.

More than just the story of my life, what you have here in your hands is my way of describing my experience with faith, and how God has been a part of this journey ever since those childhood days when I'd get down on my knees and pray.

When I talk about God, I'm not necessarily talking about religion. To me, God is the energy and light that each of us carries—some with greater strength than others—and that carries each of us. Everything we see, everything that exists, is part of God. God is in our hearts, in each and every one of us, and only we can choose whether to open the door for Him or not. To renounce Him is to open the door to fear, perdition, and unavoidable failure. To allow Him to accompany us is to overcome those fears and conquer the world. Whatever we set our hearts or minds to, if it comes from love, we will prevail; if it comes from fear, pride, or envy, we fail.

That's how I see my life. When I am close to God and my faith is strong, everything works out—more than I could ever think possible, more than I could dream of. And during those times when I've foolishly turned away from God, my career and my personal life have suffered. Today I'm more connected to God than ever before. To grow and mature is never easy, but doing so gives us knowledge and free will.

Nothing can be more important than the love and the will to live your life while being conscious of others. My children have saved me in the same way that music did in the years before I became a father.

Currently, I'm getting ready to launch a new album and start out on a new tour that will take us to dozens of countries. I'll do what I love doing: being onstage with a guitar in my hands. I'll never stop singing and playing the guitar. I'll play for those who want to hear my music. It comes from the heart and all I want to do is share my way of looking at life.

■

I've just turned forty, and I'm enjoying life as ever before. For me, time never ceases to exist. Our life is but a small segment of our overall mission in the universe, since we will go on living forever, in different forms, as we travel through energy for all eternity. Being here, on this planet, is just one small stop in a much longer journey.

We come from the place we're born, and when we die we leave behind only our bodies. Our souls carry on with the journey, there is a greater beyond, there are other beings far beyond our atmosphere. We are not alone. It's just a matter of putting everything into perspective, taking a second look at the sky and the stars, and asking the question that people have been asking since the beginning of time: Who are we? Where do we come from? What does it all mean? Why are we here?

I think our mission on Earth is to learn how to love. Everything else blows away like dust in the wind. Love is the only thing that allows us to achieve true happiness, or any other goals we may set for ourselves.

And to go through life without faith is like navigating the oceans without a compass: you'll never get to where you want to go.

Every day represents a new opportunity to embark on new adventures and challenges. All the power we need resides in our minds and hearts. Unplugging yourself from reality for a moment and elevating your consciousness is an important exercise for overcoming the state of crisis in which we live. It's easier than you might think—you just have to stop focusing on the material world. There are other levels of evolution that aren't necessarily dictated by technology or science, but by your eternal search for happiness. And it's the desired happiness that gets lost and confounded with material things.

Throughout this journey of music and faith, I have come to understand that not only are we not alone, but neither can we get anywhere alone. Everything—absolutely everything, whether we like it or not—is tightly interconnected.

My experience with art has been transformational. It has allowed me to understand the world in a new and different manner, everything from feelings to the creation of dreams to the mission of bringing happiness and hearts together.

Art is perhaps the greatest weapon of peace that we have in our hands and with which we can transform the collective imagination. Art sensitizes us, it creates awareness, and hopefully one day this will reach the people who govern us, so they will no longer see this vision as an impossible dream. I hope for a day when politics can mix with art so that everything and everyone can be purified once and for all. Today's world is disoriented and out of control. Yet it's beginning a powerful transitional period that will take years to complete, but ultimately will change the system in which we live.

This transformation may not take place during my lifetime, or my kids' lifetimes, or even in my grandchildren's lifetimes. But someday, maybe in a few hundred years, everything will have changed. There is no possible way this world can withstand another couple centuries at this pace.

There is a gradually emerging awareness. There are many beings of light out there, while others have great power and little light. Those are the ones we have to do something about. We have to change their opinions, not judge them.

This is the world in which we live: a world where very few have it all and where so many have nothing. All forms of government are imperfect, and they will remain so until the structural pillars cease to be about money and power.

The gargantuan corrupt institutions—true evidence of the corruption of men—want to show us life as it shouldn't be, happiness as it shouldn't be.

As long as the few control the many, democracy cannot exist, for democracy itself has been an unlikely experiment up to this point. If we have the technology and money to send rockets to the moon and Mars, why can't we send food to Africa? We haven't been able to overcome our own differences here on Earth, and yet we think we can go out and conquer the universe . . . Our pride continues its mischievous ways. The global population continues to grow, and yet there is less and less food and clean water to go around. I have to ask myself, how much longer can we continue living like this?

As for me, I'm doing what I believe I was brought to this world to do: to create music that raises awareness, renews hearts, and generates change. I'll continue looking to the stars and traveling the globe as God permits me. And I hope I have many years left to connect through art, to play my guitar, and to continue chasing the sun.

ACKNOWLEDGMENTS

Thank you to my family, my dear mother, my brothers and sisters, and my fans, because with them I write these pages, with them I write my life, and it is because of them that I have a voice.

PHOTO CREDITS